Hugo P. Goodwin,
3534 Pater ave,
July 9, 09.

The Music Lover's Library

The Opera Past and Present

An Historical Sketch

By

William Foster Apthorp

Author of "Musicians and Music-Lovers," Etc.

With Portraits

Charles Scribner's Sons

New York :: :: :: 1901

Trow Directory
Printing and Bookbinding Company
New York

TO

B. J. LANG

Preface

FOR a History of Opera — covering, as it does, over three centuries in four countries —to be brought within the compass of a volume like this, it must be either one of two things: something little better than a time-table, an annotated list of names and dates, or else a compendious sketch. The former plan might be excusably followed in a school text - book; though some grave doubts of its advisability might be entertained, even there. But, in a book that hopes to be read otherwise than under compulsion, it would be a self-stultifying impertinence. The other plan, of making the History a compendious sketch, is the only one to the purpose.

In writing the present Historical Sketch of the Opera, I have thrown the whole weight of my endeavour upon giving a clear and connected account of the first establishment and gradual evolution of this form of art, and upon pointing out the general quasi-philosophical rationale of the same. I have, accordingly, considered different schools, composers and works far more with reference to the influence exerted by them in furthering, or retarding, this evolution than to their intrinsic excellence. I have let the historical scythe swing high, cutting off only the most significant heads; and the most significant have not always been those the world calls greatest.

Only in two instances have I departed from this general plan: in the cases of Mozart and Beethoven. The puissant genius of these men was too closely in harmony with the fundamental idea of the Opera for them to be negligible, although they exerted infinitely little influence upon either their contemporaries or their successors in this field of composition. Of two other men, again,—Alessandro Scarlatti and Handel,—I have said extremely, perhaps surprisingly, little. Though the greatness of their genius is beyond doubt, the part they played in the history of Opera was at once unimportant and, as far as it went, antagonistic to the real evolution of the form.

Far too much importance has, it seems to me, been hitherto attributed to Scarlatti, as what may be called an *evolutionary force* in Opera. He merely propagated the influence of Giacomo Carissimi — as it had been transmitted to the seventeenth-century Venetians through Marc' Antonio Cesti, and through the Venetians to Francesco Provenzale in Naples. It may even be doubted whether the title of "Founder of the Neapolitan School," so often bestowed upon Scarlatti, do not properly belong to Provenzale. And it may be well to say here, by the way of Scarlatti's continuing the Carissimi influence, that Romain Rolland seems to have dealt rather a severe blow to the legend that he was Carissimi's pupil, in establishing the fact that he studied under Provenzale — a man of extraordinary genius, whom Rolland may fairly be said to have rediscovered for the benefit of a too forgetful world. For forty-six years Carissimi had been living without intermission in Rome, as *Maestro di cappella* at S. Apollinare, when he died there in 1674; Scarlatti was born only fifteen years before this, in 1659, at Trapani in Sicily. The proximity of these dates, and the distance between the two places, make it at least improbable that the one man ever studied under the other; at most, Scarlatti could only have begun his education under Carissimi. Furthermore, the hypothesis of his having been Carissimi's pupil is not needed to account for his spreading that master's influence; for this influence was already the dominant one over Opera when Scarlatti first came upon the field. He may have transferred a remaining musical form or two, which had been established by Carissimi, from the Oratorio to the Opera; but such transfers had been made so copiously by his Venetian predecessors, that not much, if anything, can have been left for him to do in that line.

Succinctly stated, the main object of the present volume is this: To show how a general desire for some such form of dramatico-lyric art as the Opera was manifested in France and Italy considerably before any possibility existed of its coming into actual being; how this possibility was at last realized by the devising of a style of artistic monodic composition by the Florentine Music Reform, and how the Opera itself was among the first practical results of that Reform. That the theoretical principles in accordance with which the Opera was first established in Florence, in 1595, were essentially identical with those promulgated in the nineteenth century by Richard Wagner. That the Opera was first diverted from its original artistic purpose through the influence of Carissimi, and, from being an essentially dramatic and scenic form of art, became a purely musical one. And finally, how this Carissimi influence continued to make itself felt, even through and in spite of the Gluck reaction against it, until Wagner at last gave it its death-blow.

In telling the story of this long warfare between two opposite principles,—the original Florentine dramatic one, and the Carissimi anti-dramatic,—I have, with the two exceptions mentioned above, considered only such men as took a prominent active part in the fight, and more especially such as fought on the dramatic side. For the history of this conflict is really the history of Opera. Looked at from this point of view, some of the greatest geniuses, like Scarlatti, and even Handel himself,—who had it all their own way, their party being so much in the ascendant at the time that there was virtually no opposition,—are seen to be of less importance than, say, a man like Rossini,—who, after arrogantly fighting on the wrong side when he ought to have known (and did know) better, gave at least one mighty blow for the right, — or even a mediocrity like Giovanni Pacini,—who, in his mild way, did some fighting in the good cause. Of the men who dealt no blows on either side, or whose feeble strokes left no mark, nothing has been said.

I should perhaps say a word or two in explanation of my dwelling so almost exclusively upon the tragic, or "high-romantic" forms of Opera, and saying so little about the comic. I had two reasons for this. In the first place, the comic forms—*opera buffa*, *opéra-comique*, *Singspiel*—have everywhere been the distinctly national ones throughout; the tragic, or romantic forms,—*opera seria*, *tragédie-lyrique*, and Grand Opera in general,—the more universal, the more cosmopolitan. Then, the influence of the comic forms upon the development of the tragic, or romantic, has been generally but slight; whereas the converse influence has often been very noteworthy. And I have taken the more influential and cosmopolitan forms as the more important.

For a similar reason I have omitted all consideration of the development of the Opera outside of Italy, France, Germany, and England. What developments it has had in Spain, Scandinavia, Russia, Hungary, or Bohemia have had no influence whatever upon the rest of the world. What these countries have done in Opera has, it is true, often reflected foreign influences, but has not exerted any frontier-crossing influence of its own in return. Perhaps, on this principle, all reference to Opera in England might have been omitted as well; but we are Anglo - Saxons, and the subject touches us more near.

I wish to express my deep obligation to the admirable articles on *Monteverdi* and *Marco da Gagliano* by E. VOGEL in the Leipzig *Viertel-jahrsschrift für Musikwissenschaft* (Vols. III. and V.), to the article in the same publication (Vol. VIII.) on *Die venezianische Oper und die Werke Cavalli's und Cesti's* by HERMANN KRETZSCHMAR, and to ROMAIN ROLLAND'S *Les origines du théâtre lyrique moderne ; histoire de l'Opéra en Europe avant Lully et Scarlatti* (Paris, 1895) for a great deal in the first two chapters of this volume. Vogel's and Rolland's careful and energetic research has, indeed, considerably topsy - turvied previous histories of the Florentine and Venetian periods of the Opera. For the rest of the volume, I have relied, partly upon older standard authorities, but mainly upon my own investigations—especially in the matter of criticism.

W. F. A.

BOSTON, December 13, 1900.

Contents

Portraits

THE OPERA

Past and Present

A truly princely spectacle, and delightful beyond all others, being one in which are combined all the most noble oblectations, such as contrivance and interest of plot, diction, style, mellifluous rhyme, musical art, the concert of voices and instruments, excellency in singing, grace in dancing and gesture ; and it may also be said that painting plays therein no unimportant part, in the matters of scenery and costume ; so that the intellect and every noblest sentiment are fascinated at one and the same moment by the most delectable arts ever devised by human genius.

MARCO DA GAGLIANO, Preface to *Dafne*.

The Music Lover's Library

WAGNER.

I

Beginnings

LET us take the Egyptians and Assyrians for granted; enough that the consociation of the arts of Poetry, Music, and Dancing in the Drama dates back at least to <u>Thespis's cart</u>. How intimate the union of these three arts may have been in the classic Greek Drama, and its later Roman imitation, is a question little to our present purpose; for, though all three still had a place in what remained of the Drama in the Middle Ages, they were bound together by no intimate bond of union. Of that, so to speak, "chemical" union of this <u>clover-leaf of arts</u>, of that mutually helpful coöperation toward a common dramatic end, which is the essence of Opera, nothing was to be found. And, as just this coöperative union is the essence of Opera, as a special form of dramatic art, it is evident that the Opera could not come into being until such an union had been established, or—supposing it really to have existed in the old Greek Drama—re-established.

3

The Opera Past and Present

A drama with incidental music is not an opera; such dramas were not uncommon long before anything like Opera was known. The type of Drama which we now know as *vaudeville*—a play interspersed with songs—is to be recognized in the old French satire-plays and dramatic pastorals. A noteworthy example is Adam de la Halle's *Li gieus de Robin et de Marion*, given at the court of Charles d'Artois in Naples, probably in 1285. This little pastoral-play was long looked upon as the first opera in history, and the trouvère Adam de la Halle, as the first opera-composer. Unluckily for this time-honoured distinction, recent research has proved beyond a doubt that neither the music nor the text of the songs was written by Adam, but only the connecting dialogue. As was the fashion of the day, he took a certain number of popular ballads, constructed a dramatic story out of them, and bound them together into a play with spoken dialogue of his own invention. The thing can not be called an opera, but, at the very most, an operatic symptom. Neither was it the first nor last of its kind.

That playwrights and musicians—especially the latter—had a vague premonition of something like Opera long before they had the means of writing one, is more than likely. What may be called premonitory symptoms of Opera were

4

not uncommon in the musical and dramatic life of the Middle Ages and the earlier Renaissance period; they became especially recognizable as symptomatic about the middle of the sixteenth century, both in France and Italy. One finds a distinct yearning after Opera, and manifold attempts to create something as nearly like it as possible. Furthermore, some of these attempts show plainly, not only a desire on the part of musicians to do something operatic, but also a total lack of adequate means of satisfying this desire at the time.

Leaving the Art of Dancing out of consideration, for the moment, as of secondary theoretic importance, we can see that nothing like Opera was possible, so long as the Art of Music was in no condition to fulfil, not only certain dramatic, but also (and more especially) certain scenic requirements. Such scenic requirements were, to be sure, fulfilled to some extent by the folk-song or popular ballad; but this form of music, as then practised, had no dramatic character. Moreover, the folk-song lay outside the then domain of what would be called artistic composition; technically well-trained musicians who had an ambition to be recognized as composers would have nothing to do with it; at best, they would take a folk-song, as they would a Gregorian chaunt, as material to be worked

up in strict counterpoint—which latter was
the only form of *soi-disant* " artistic " composition known at the time. And counterpoint
was essentially polyphonic—in several interwoven voices, or parts—and, as such, absolutely unfit for all but an exceedingly limited
range of scenic uses. In a composition for the
concert-room a polyphonic or choral passage
may, at a pinch, stand for the utterance of a
single individual; * but it can not do so on the
dramatic stage. A single actor can not sing in
four or five parts (" real " or otherwise), and to
put a visible quartet or quintet of singers upon
the stage, to impersonate a single individual,
would be a slap in the face of dramatic realism
against which even the most imaginatively disposed audience would protest.

So composers who wished to write dramatic
music — counterpoint being the only known
medium—had perforce to forego actual dramatic representation of their works, and content
themselves with performances in the concert-
room. But let no one think contrapuntal po-
lyphony an impossible vehicle for dramatic expression. True, strict vocal counterpoint in
the old modal system, quite devoid of sighing

---

* Modern instances of this sort of thing are not wanting. Mendelssohn, in his *Paulus*, makes the Lord speak in a four-part
chorus of female voices.

or yearning chromatics, does not seem a very poignantly expressive medium to us now; but there resided in it at least some expressive potentialities, which the then composers were eager to make the most of; in any case, the will was not wanting. Indeed, an ever-growing tendency to lay stress upon the intentional expression of definite emotion is noticeable in the great contrapuntists of the fifteenth and sixteenth centuries, from old Josquin Després (1450–1521) down; and from the emotionally expressive to the dramatic is but a step.

The early madrigal-plays—what we should call dramatic cantatas—in France and Italy were really far more significant operatic symptoms than the older stage-plays of the *Robin et Marion* sort, even though these latter were given with scenery, costumes, and dramatic action on a real stage. Although written for the concert-room, the madrigal-plays showed a distinct striving on the part of composers to do something more dramatic with music than had been done theretofore, which the *vaudeville*-like stage-plays did not in the least.

It is noteworthy that, especially in Italy, these madrigal-plays generally took a comic direction. Alessandro Striggio of Mantua (1535–1584) writes a series of rustic scenes for four and five voices, carrying the listener

Early. Madrigal Plays.

7

through the various occurrences of a village day: scenes of village gossip and scandal, servants' complaints of their masters, bickerings and hand-to-hand fight of washerwomen, reconciliation, kisses, and sunset. Giovanni Croce of Chioggia (1550–1609) sets the whole Venetian carnival to music, often with no little realistic *vis comica*. At last we come to the comic cantatas of Orazio Vecchi of Modena (1551–1605) and his pupil, Adriano Banchieri of Bologna (1567–1634). These were sung on the stage by costumed singers; the text was a regular play, but there was no acting, and the music of each *dramatis persona* was for from three to five voices, quite in the traditional contrapuntal madrigal style, but often overbrimming with picturesque suggestiveness and comic realism. These cantatas represent the dramatic culmination of the old modal counterpoint, the last stage of the preliminary evolution which preceded the advent of Opera in Italy.

Equally symptomatic, if in a different way, were some of the developments of the court ballet in France under the Valois. The ballet, as in favour at the French court about the middle of the sixteenth century, was essentially what we should now call a *ballet d'action;* it was based on some timely theme, generally of

8

a classico-mythological character, and this central idea was developed in recited verses, songs, choruses, dancing, and pantomime, often with the aid of very ingenious stage-machinery. The scheme was artless enough, the thing had little dramatic consistency; but the elements of poetry, music, dancing, and dramatic action were here associated together, and the bond of union between all four was not so loose but that a light touch of the magician's wand would suffice to turn the whole thing into Opera. The eye of History even descries something very like that magician in Balthasar de Beaujoyeulx, a Piedmontese violinist—his real name was Baltazarini—who came to Paris with a company of Italian fiddlers in 1577, being recommended by the maréchal de Brissac to Catherine de Médicis; she made him her *valet de chambre*. This Beaujoyeulx associated with himself several court poets, musicians, and painters * in organizing a grand ballet called *Circé, ou le ballet comique de la Reine*, which was given by Henri III in the salle des cariatides of the palais du Petit-Bourbon on Sunday, October 15, 1581, in honour of the marriage of the duc de Joyeuse and Marguerite de Vaudémont de

* La Chesnaye, de Beaulieu, Maistre Salmon, Jacques Patin, Desportes, Baïf, Ronsard, and Th. Agrippa d'Aubigné are mentioned as having a hand in it.

Lorraine, the queen's sister.* The plot was of
the simplest: a gentleman, hastening to an-
nounce the reign of Peace and Plenty to His
Most Christian Majesty, is waylaid by Circé,
and by her changed into a lion. Half the gods
and goddesses of Olympus, not to mention other
mythological personages, try to liberate him,
but either return discomfited to whence they
came, or are likewise transformed into beasts.
At last the Royal Word does the business, and
all ends happily. The whole is interspersed
with harangues,—distilling an amount of court
holy-water suggestive of His Most Christian
Majesty's having a fine stomach for adulation,—
songs, duets, choruses, instrumental intermez-
zi, and two grand ballet-interludes.† The per-

plot
Circé

---

* BALTHASAR DE BEAUJOYEULX, *Balet comyque de la Royne.*
Paris: Adrien Le Roy, Ballard et Mamert Pattison, 1582.

BEAUJOYEULX, *le Ballet comique de la Reine*, etc., reconstitué
et réduit pour piano et chant par J.-B. WECKERLIN. Paris:
Théodore Michaëlis, *s. d.*

A copy of the former (the original full score) is now in the Bibli-
othèque Nationale in Paris; one of Weckerlin's pianoforte-score is
in the Boston Public Library.

† One little strain of the music has come down to our day: the
last nine measures of ballet-music in the first interlude, taken from
an old song, *le Son de la clochette*, which, under the name of
Amaryllis, used to be a favourite at Mr. Thomas's concerts in
New York and elsewhere, in an arrangement by one Ghys—who
wrongly attributed its composition to Henri III himself. The
song is much older than the last of the Valois.

formance was probably the most sumptuous on record, lasted from ten o'clock in the evening to a half after three in the morning, "without anyone's noticing its length," and cost over 1,200,000 *écus*.* The curious reader can find a detailed account of its scenic splendours of solid gold, silver, and real gems—Circé's Garden, Golden Vault, Grove of Pan, Fountain of Glaucus, etc.—its gorgeously attired court beauties and professional singers, in Celler.† The experiment was too expensive to be repeated!

What differentiates the *Ballet de la Reine* from the many court ballets that preceded it under the Valois, and followed it under the Bourbons, is its superior consistency of dramatic plot; possibly also an occasional dramatic accent in the music. If not quite a full-fledged opera, —Celler is a little over-anxious to accept it as one,—it was more like an opera than anything that came before it in France. Call it at least an "opera in embryo," a noteworthy premonitory symptom of what was to come. As such, one of the most remarkable things about it was

---

* If this means silver *écus*, the sum would be 3,600,000 francs; if gold, 6,000,000 francs. Say, from $720,000 to $1,200,000 of our money.

† LUDOVIC CELLER, *Les origines de l'Opéra et le Ballet de la Reine*, Paris: Didier et Cie., 1868.

the wholly unpremeditated way Baltazarini stumbled, as it were, upon a style of musico-dramatic entertainment so very like what French Opera was destined to become in after years; this seems to have been, with him, a matter of pure clairvoyant instinct.

So far had matters been brought forward in the operatic direction by the last quarter of the sixteenth century; all that opera-thirsty musicians were still waiting for was a form of music that could be put to scenic uses. That form once found, the Opera would come of itself!

About the last decade of the century a coterie of Florentine nobles made a noteworthy discovery. This was virtually that, though the Renaissance in Art and Literature was hard upon two centuries old, the Art of Music had been quite untouched by it. This isolated position of Music during over a century and a half of the Renaissance may seem strange, but was really entirely natural, even unavoidable.

The whole Renaissance movement was essentially a return to the Classic, a setting up of antique theory and practice as unquestioned guides in matters of Art and Literature. Now, it was comparatively easy for the promoters of the Renaissance to take up Painting, Sculpture, Architecture, Poetry, and Literature in general where the ancient Greeks and Romans had left them ; these arts had been lying fallow through the Middle Ages, utterly neglected; the thread could be knotted together again, and the evolution proceed almost as if there had been no break. But with Music this was impossible. The Art of Music had not shared the long torpid sleep of her sister arts during the Middle Ages, but, from the tenth century on, had been pursuing a course of evolution of her own, and, what is more, a course of evolution almost wholly uninfluenced by antique precept or example. By the time the Renaissance began, this evolution had made giant strides. So the promoters of the Renaissance, who found the other arts lying torpid and, like Rip Van Winkle, no farther advanced than when they had first gone to sleep, found Music very wide awake indeed, with four centuries of formal evolution already behind her. Moreover, as this evolution had been hardly influenced at all by classic principles, it was no wonder that the art had got into a condition which made classic precepts utterly inapplicable. The writings of Plato, Aristotle, and other ancient philosophers —the infallible Bibles of the Renaissance æsthetic creed—were infinitely instructive about Painting, Sculpture, Architecture, and Poetry; but they had nothing whatever to say about strict vocal counterpoint, the one musical form

which the four centuries of evolution had
brought forth. Counterpoint was clearly irre-
deemably un-Platonic and un-Aristotelian, and
that was the self-evident long and short of it!

That our Florentine friends should have
waked up one fine morning to this damning
fact—damning, for to be un-Hellenic was to
be inartistic—is not surprising; it would have
been more astonishing, had they remained
longer blind to it. But, once awake to this
fact, they determined to act upon it forthwith.
They instituted the so-called Florentine Music-
Reform of the seventeenth century—a movement of importance in history. The true gist
of this reform was to bring the Art of Music for
the first time under the sway of Renaissance
principles; it was the Renaissance of the art.

These reformers were Giovanni Bardi, a distinguished Della-Cruscan and member of the
Accademia degl' Alterati; Piero Strozzi; Vincenzo Galilei, father of "*E pur si muove*"; and
Jacopo Corsi. With these noblemen were
associated Ottavio (or Ottaviano) Rinuccini,
the poet, and two professional musicians:
Jacopo Peri, nicknamed *il Zazzerino* from his
fine shock of gold-red hair ("*bellissima capella-
tura fra bionda e rossa*"), and Giulio Caccini,
better known in his day, like his namesake the
painter, as Giulio Romano. The coterie was

14

collectively known as *la Camerata* — " the Chamber." *

The Reform was both destructive and constructive. Destructively, it was war to the knife with counterpoint, and with all for which counterpoint stood. Rather a comprehensive program, in its way ; as much so as that wholesale demand for "*l'arrestation des coquins et des lâches*" in the French National Assembly. For the abolition of counterpoint meant nothing more nor less than wiping out the only form of music then known, and nullifying all the practical technique in composition that had been acquired after four centuries of labour. Constructively, the Reform meant the devising of a new form of composition, governed by the strictest and most uncompromising antique-Hellenic principles. Music was to do nothing

---

* The dates of Peri's birth and death are not known ; he was a Florentine of humble birth, but seems somehow to have persuaded himself that he could lay just claim to descent from the noble family of Peri. Caccini, several years his junior, was born in Rome between 1558 and 1560 ; when a young man, he came to settle in Florence, where he died in 1640. Peri was a very thoroughly trained musician, decidedly more so than Caccini, who was, however, far enough from being the mere bungler some historians have called him. From the beginning, every pioneer in a new musical direction has been called a poor musician by his academic contemporaries. Both Caccini and Peri were famous singers ; Caccini was also noted as a teacher of singing.

but help to express the sentiments of the poetic text; it was to take its whole plastic form from that text—from the natural rhetorical accents of ordinary speech, the natural emotional rise and fall of the voice, from the metre of the verse, even from the very rhyme. All so-called purely musical freedom was to be denied it, it was to become the docile hand-maid of Poetry. In other words, an absolute *tabula rasa* was to be made of the whole Art of Music.

As a matter of fact, this Florentine Reform was the dawn of "artistic" monodic composition—for a single voice with instrumental accompaniment—on principles which the reader must already have recognized as strictly Wagnerian. The style of writing which the *Camerata* thus originated was called the *stile rappresentativo*, or "representative (*i.e.* expressive) style"; something very like what we now call recitative.

Kind Fortune smiled. What could, for instance, have been luckier—we having made a *tabula rasa* of the Art of Music—than the opportune publication, in 1592, of Claudio Monteverdi's third book of madrigals, an epoch-making volume, big with a whole new Tonal System, with "free dominant 7ths" and other luxuries, unheard-of before? A most fitting novelty for a new era to begin with! The point of depart-

ure for all Modern Music, did we but know it!
Then, how well our new monodic style, quite
dazzling in its Hellenic purity, fits in with that
other great factor of the Renaissance: the
growth of Individualism in Art. Really the
prime product of the whole Renaissance movement, the wheat, of which our vaunted classicism is but the chaff. For our classicism is, in
the end, but a blind, a manifesto, something to
sign and swear to; but the Individualism is a
natural, instinctive growth, and has more than
the force of signed parchment. Painters and
sculptors have, for the last half century and
more, been forswearing their allegiance to the
classic type, and limning the features of the
woman most after their own heart; poets have
sung what they themselves have seen and felt—
and let the Academy go hang. And now we
composers can do likewise in our way: turn
our backs upon the typical generalities of counterpoint, and put our inmost selves into harmony and melody. You singers, too, can at
last stand forth from the choir, and be your-
selves alone. Here, if anywhere, is a free field
for Individualism; pity only that we have no
working technique ready-made for the occasion; for the old contrapuntal technique will
surely not carry us far on our new road. But
courage! a technique has been developed once,

and can be developed again. We will enter
upon our new era of the Art of Music with
hearts undaunted, and put our forebears to the
blush yet!

Strange, though, what ideals men in an interesting condition will set up for themselves, and
how little the most ardent players see of the
game. Here was the *Camerata* with a brand-
new musical style (fondly believed by them to
be authentically antique), eminently adapted to
scenic use. And to what use, think you, did
they purpose putting it? To a revival of the
Greek Drama, the crowning consummation of
that Hellenic palingenesis which was the proud-
est boast of the Renaissance! Of all imaginable
projects, probably the most hopeless—in Italy
in the last decade of the sixteenth century.
Yet this was what the *Camerata* were bent upon
bringing about, cost what it might; and that
they could do it they had never a doubt. That
they did not do it, nor anything like it, need
hardly be said; they did better, they gave birth
to the Opera. To think that this, of all forms
of art, should owe its existence to a set of as
arrant pedants as ever drew breath!—for that
the members of the *Camerata* (always excepting
Caccini and Peri) distinctly were, pedants to
the finger-tips.

The first high festival of the new musical cult

was the performance of _Dafne—a favola in musica_, or opera, the libretto by Rinuccini, the music by Peri—at Corsi's palace in 1595. This was the first opera on record, and so successful that it was repeated at several successive carnivals. It was written in the _stile rappresentativo_; yet hear what Pietro della Valle (a most competent witness) wrote afterwards about the singing of Vittoria Archilei, who took the part of Dafne: "She was no beauty, but the foremost songstress of the time. She ornamented the written monody with long flourishes and turns (_lunghi giri e gruppi_) which disfigured it, but were much in fashion, and the singer Peri praises them highly." * So, at the very first dawn of Opera did the virtuoso singer have her share in the business, and have her "disfiguring" flourishes condoned by the composer! The fact is not without its significance. †

The score of _Dafne_ has been lost; all the performances were in private, before invited audiences. But the Opera made its official, public entry into the world five years later.

---

* In a letter to Lelio Guidiccioni, January 16, 1640—forty and odd years after the performance; but some men have tenacious memories. Note, too, that "the singer Peri" was the composer himself.

† _Vide_ Peri's preface to _Euridice_ in Appendix, page 221.

By order of the grand duke, Rinuccini wrote the libretto of *Euridice;* it was set to music separately by both Caccini and Peri, each composer writing his own complete score. The opera was given, as part of the festivities in honour of the wedding of Henri IV, of France, and Maria de' Medici, in the Pitti Palace on October 6, 1600; at this first performance part of Peri's music and part of Caccini's were given. But both scores were published separately.

In Caccini's and Peri's *Euridices* we have fair samples of what serious Italian Opera was in its first estate. There are some few choruses in the madrigal style; the dialogue is all carried on in the *stile rappresentativo*. But many vocal flourishes are actually written down, especially in Caccini's score, so they can not be charged to any whim of the Archilei, who sang the part of Euridice, unless, indeed, she exerted some personal influence over the composers, who, between pedantic noble patrons, on the one hand, and an indispensable prima donna, on the other, may well have had moments of doubt as to which was the devil and which the deep sea.

Yet this personal influence, though quite supposable, is not necessary to account for the flourishes; it is more than probable that Caccini and Peri would have written them in any event. They, men of original genius, must have felt that Music, as the idealizing element in Opera, ought to be treated with something of ideality. Now, it happens that the idealizing power of this mysterious Art of Tones resides in its sensuous beauty of line and colour; and, owing to the primordial, amorphous condition into which the Reform had thrown Music,—with counterpoint abolished, the orchestra merely rudimentary, tonal harmony in its infancy, and true melody unborn,—well-nigh the only sensuous appeal to the musical ear they had at command was that of florid vocalization by a beautiful voice. Those long "*giri e gruppi*" were the sacrifice they forced the stern *stile rappresentativo* to offer up at the altar of musical beauty and ideality.

Thus was the Opera born: of a determined, if utterly foolish and futile, attempt to revive the classic Greek Drama in the last decade of the sixteenth century in Florence. It entered upon life with its dramatic side very perfectly developed,—for Rinuccini was distinctly a man of genius, both as poet and dramatist; far above the average of his day, one of the best librettists ever known,—with its musical side in a merely embryonic condition. Yet the music, in one respect, quite fulfilled the demands of the most nineteenth-century æsthetics: in its absolute

[margin note: Reason for florid Song.]

subserviency to the emotional expression of the text, in its thoroughly scenic quality, its allowing the actor the completest practicable freedom of dramatic action. In other words, the Opera began (in theory, at least) as a perfect exemplification of the art principles of the Wagnerian Music-Drama; all that was lacking was a further musical development.*

---

* Peri's claim to being the Father of the Opera has been disputed. It is known that Emilio del Cavaliere (or de' Cavalieri)— a Roman nobleman (born about 1550, died before 1600) who came to Florence between 1570 and 1580, and held the post of Inspector-General of Art and Artists under Ferdinando de' Medici up to 1596—wrote music to three plays, two of which—*Il Satiro* and *La disperazione di Fileno*—were given on the stage in 1590, that is, four years before Peri's *Dafne*. The whole question rests on the character of the music to these plays, the scores of which have been lost. Peri plainly refers to them in his preface to *Euridice* (*vide* Appendix), but in a way that is open to more than one interpretation. The expression "our Music (*nostra Musica*)" might be taken to mean the *stile rappresentativo* of the *Camerata ;* but it is known that del Cavaliere had no connection with the *Camerata*. Moreover, Peri's subsequent statement that he himself (who certainly did write in the *stile rappresentativo*) had treated the text "in a different manner (*in altra guisa*)" contradicts this. Upon the whole, considering the fashions of the day, may not the "our Music," as well as the "with marvellous originality," have been sheer bits of conventional flattery, quite natural for an artist like Peri to use in referring to a nobleman of del Cavaliere's influence in Florence, especially as that nobleman, not belonging to the *Camerata*, might be well worth propitiating ? In those days it was difficult to gather a man's real meaning from what he said in a dedicatory preface.

II

The European Conquest

THE first to follow the Florentine lead, and trump all the *Camerata's* aces, were Claudio Monteverdi and Marco da Gagliano.*

Monteverdi was born at Cremona in May, 1567, and studied under Marc' Antonio Ingegnieri, *maestro di cappella* at the cathedral. From 1590 to 1612 he was in the service of Vincenzo Gonzaga, duke of Mantua, at first as singer and violist, then as *maestro di cappella* and court com-

---

* The first composer's name is spelt *Monteverdo* in the baptismal register. On the title-pages of most of his published works it stands as *Monteverde ;* once as *Monte Verde.* But the 113 autograph letters that have come down to us are, without exception, signed *Monteverdi.* This plural termination is undoubtedly the right one. *Vide* VOGEL, *Claudio Monteverdi,* in *Vierteljahrsschrift für Musikwissenschaft,* III., 315.

Da Gagliano's name is given wrong in most cyclopædias. The error has been traced to F.-J. Fétis, who, seeing "Marco di Zanobi da Gagliano" in an article by Picchianti in the *Gazetta musicale di Milano* (1844, No. 1), mistook *Zanobi* for the family surname, and the *di* for a sign of noblesse. *Zanobi* was the Christian name of Marco's father, and the family was so far from noble that its surname has never come to light. *Vide Ib.,* V.

poser; from 1613 to his death, on November 29, 1643, he was *maestro di cappella* at St. Mark's in Venice. He was one of the greatest geniuses, probably the very greatest pioneer, in the whole history of Music. We have already met him as the discoverer of the modern Tonal System—a discovery which revolutionized the whole Art of Music; he developed the ponderous, unwieldy *stile rappresentativo* of the *Camerata*, with its leaden accompaniment in long-sustained notes, into the more vivacious and passionate *stile concitato* (or " excited style "), letting the accompaniment take its own rhythm and strike as many repeated notes to the measure as he pleased, thus establishing the basis for nearly all modern writing for a voice, or voices, with instrumental accompaniment. This repercussion of notes, pushed to the due degree of speed, became the string *tremolo*—a device against which the players kicked lustily at first, as physically impossible. He also invented the string *pizzicato*. The whole great Art of Instrumentation owes its origin to him. He and da Gagliano carried the Opera one stage farther in its musical development; not a very long stage, perhaps, but none the less an important one. They threw Dramatic Music, already big with Melody, into her travail-throes; the whole dramatic style showed greater freedom and mastery.

[handwritten marginalia: Monteverdi / Orfeo. 160]

On May 28, 1607, Monteverdi's first opera, *Orfeo* (the libretto by Alessandro Striggio), was given with great success at the *Accademia degl' Invaghiti* in Mantua. Toward the end of January, 1608, it was followed by da Gagliano's *Dafne* (Rinuccini's old libretto, revamped for the occasion by the author), given in honour of the duke's youngest son, Ferdinando Gonzaga, being made cardinal. On May 28 of the same year came the most overwhelming success of all, Monteverdi's *Arianna* (the text by Rinuccini), given to celebrate the nuptials of Francesco Gonzaga (the eldest son) and Margherita di Savoia.

In Monteverdi's *Orfeo* we find Caccini and Peri left well behind. The monody has more musical independence, a freer dramatic fire; the orchestration begins to assume an importance of its own; the harmony is richer and more appositely expressive; in short, one feels a stronger hand at the bellows.* All that remains of *Arianna* is one monologue, Arianna's famous lament, "*Lasciatemi morire!*" after being abandoned by Teseo. No single composition was ever more famous in its day than this *Lamento;* contemporary letters are rich in ac-

[handwritten marginalia: famous lament]

---

* It is rather curious that, of all Monteverdi's opera-scores, only the first and last—*Orfeo* (Mantua, 1607) and *L'Incoronatione di Poppea* (Venice, 1642)—have been preserved.

counts of its pathetic beauty and of the overwhelming impression it made upon all listeners.
Even to-day we can feel its enormous dramatic
power, its wondrous truth and depth of pathos.*

So far, the Opera had been distinctly aristocratic, a *bonne bouche* for cultivated *cognoscenti*;
but a change was soon to come. In 1637 the
first public opera-house—Teatro di San Cassiano †—was opened in Venice; with it, the
Opera was brought for the first time face to
face with the great general public. Thence-
forth the people—together with, but quite as
much as, crowned heads and affluent nobles—
were to be arbiters of its destiny. And, as Hans
Sachs says,

> Wer Preise erkennt, und Preise stellt,
> der will am End' auch dass man ihm gefällt.‡

That the Opera must come down from its high
perch of pseudo-Hellenic purism, and appeal to
a taste quite other than that of a cultivated
aristocracy, was evident enough.

---

* It is printed entire, omitting the short choruses between the
stanzas, in VOGEL, *ubi sup.*, 445–450; unfortunately the accompaniment is given only in figured bass.

† Most Venetian opera-houses were named after the nearest
church.

‡ Freely Englished: " He who offers and awards prizes likes,
upon the whole, to be pleased in his own way."—*Die Meistersinger von Nürnberg*, Act III., scene 2.

Accordingly we find, in this Venetian period of the Lyric Drama, a marked deterioration in the character of libretti. Classico-mythological subjects make way for classico-historical ones; historical only in title and in the names of the *dramatis personæ*, for the whole social and moral atmosphere is seventeenth-century Venetian; high-buskinned Tragedy quits the field, to make room for the intrigues and loud fustian of Melodrama. Almost the only theme is intrigue: intrigue amorous, intrigue political, intrigue villainous; the favourite hinge to the plot is what the French call *travestissement*, disguise in somebody else's clothes; all the characters, noble or base, virtuous or debauched, patriotic or traitorous, have, as Romain Rolland acutely remarks, one trait in common: they invariably seek to gain their several ends by lying! Side by side with the most hair-raising sophistications of rhetoric and metaphor, we find a naïveté as of Navahoes and Zunis; for ingenuous anachronisms, these opera-texts put Shakspere to the blush.* Last, but not least, the comic personage, the low comedian dear to the gods, makes his way upon the stage, flouting heroes

---

* For instance, Praxiteles accompanies Phryne to a "solemn fair" in Athens, where, after expatiating upon the products of "Asia, America (*sic!*), Europe, Africa, and the world," he buys her a "gold watch."

and demigods with his tart wit. The Opera is popularizing itself with a vengeance!

And with this popular movement comes success; for, as George Eliot says, "none but the ancients could be always classic." After the San Cassiano, opera-house upon opera-house is opened in Venice; by the end of the century there are eleven of them in full blast—a generous allowance for a population of about 140,000. What a cultivated aristocracy thought of the business is not reported; but it probably did not kick over-hard, and may, in its heart of heart, have been not disinclined to welcome a respite from being "always classic." But that impressive spectre of a revived Greek Drama was sent back to limbo for good and all! Upon the whole, whatever the Opera may have lost in dignity by thus tumbling down from its aristocratic-classical perch, it certainly gained in vigour and pithiness by becoming a frank expression of the Spirit of the Age.

The ruling individuality of this whole Venetian period of the Opera was Monteverdi's greatest pupil, Cavalli. Pier-Francesco Caletti-Bruni was born at Crema, near Venice, in 1599 or 1600; his father was *maestro di cappella* at the church of Sta. Maria in Crema. He was taken to Venice by Federigo Cavalli, a Venetian nobleman and *podestà* of the province of Crema, who lodged him in his own house and had him educated as a musician. The boy was soon popularly known as *il Checo di Câ-Cavalli* (Franky of the house of Cavalli), and his real name was gradually dropped. As composer, as organist (1665) and *maestro di cappella* (1668) at St. Mark's, he was always known as Francesco Cavalli.

Cavalli's was a rugged, passionate, wholly masculine nature; with a lightning-flash of instinct he would dive to the bottom of a dramatic situation, and, without any reflective process, crystallise out its gist in a few measures of matchless music. He was fond of rapid, brilliant strokes, hitting the nail upon the head and driving it home at a blow. There is something Wagnerish in the heroic pomp of his style, in the laconic pithiness of an occasional trumpet-like theme; more Wagnerish still is his glowing picturesque imaginativeness. He for the first time brought something of the popular song into Opera; his fondness for simple, concise melodic forms is conspicuous. He welcomed the laughable personage upon the lyric stage, and treated him musically with consummate mastery. A born son of the people, he was just the man to give convincing expression to the popular spirit.

Of Cavalli's thirty-nine operas, the first, *Le*

nozze di Teti e Peleo, was brought out at the San Cassiano in 1639; the last, a second version of *Erismena*, at the San Salvatore in 1670. His best and most famous works were probably *Giasone* (San Cassiano, 1649) and *Ercole* (Paris, 1662). He died in Venice on January 14, 1676.

The introduction of the comic element into Opera—which may be roughly dated with Cavalli's *Doriclea* (San Cassiano, 1645)—was one of the most noteworthy features of the earlier part of the Venetian movement; it was, in the best sense, popular. Another innovation was less good: the gradual discarding of the chorus —probably chiefly for financial reasons, the salaries of leading artists having much increased since the first opera-houses were opened. In other parts of Italy the comic and satirical Opera flourished almost to the exclusion of the more serious form. The *opera buffa* was fast coming into vogue. Nowhere, save in Mantua (and at first in Venice), was the ultra-classicism of the *Camerata* accepted; either the purely comic and satirical variety was taken as the standard norm, or else the mixed serio-comic one, as developed in Venice by Cavalli. Especially in Naples was this latter cultivated, with both the comic and the melodramatic elements pushed to artless exaggeration.

The chief figure in the, so to speak, preli-

minary period of Opera in Naples—before the
more characteristic " great " (or " beautiful ")
Neapolitan period—was Francesco Provenzale,
one of the greatest and most forgotten geniuses
in the history of Opera, suspected by Romain
Rolland to be identical with the better-known
Francesco della Torre. He was born about
1610, and died no one knows when. His *La
Stellidaura vendicata* (1670), *Il schiavo di sua
moglie* (1671), and — if Rolland's suspicion is
right—*Alessandro Bala* (1678) show him to have
been a consummate master of the serio-comic
style, with, however, a strong leaning toward
the tragic.

If the Venetian movement could but have
continued longer in its original direction, the
whole subsequent history of Opera might have
been different; the form might gradually have
outgrown its melodramatic frivolities, and
have become in time the highest and most natural sort of Lyric Drama. But this was not
to be ; a new element was suddenly introduced,
which straightway, and all but permanently,
changed the whole face of the matter.

Up to about the middle of Cavalli's career,
the whole progressive development of the
Opera had been of the musical sort ; considering the dramatic perfection and musical pri-
mitiveness of the form in its first estate, under

the Florentine *Camerata*, this was inevitable. But, as Mr. Runciman well says, no one learns how to do a thing best by trying to do something else; it is easy to see how a new musical evolution could be pushed forward more freely and rapidly by composers who did not write for the stage than by opera-writers who were unavoidably hampered by scenic considerations. To make Music musical is one thing; to make it musical and scenic at the same time is a double task. No wonder, then, that the undramatic composers soon outstripped their opera-writing contemporaries.

Giacomo Carissimi (born at Marino, near Rome, about 1604, died in Rome in 1674), unquestionably the greatest genius of his time in Music, had done mighty work in developing the Oratorio. Indeed, this wonderful man did virtually the work of a whole century in the matter of formal musical evolution; he developed and established wellnigh every form of vocal composition cultivated in Bach's and Handel's day. He never wrote for the stage; and the musical forms he developed did not in any way take the stage into account.

In 1649 * his favourite pupil, Marc' Antonio

* At least, Cesti's *Orontea* was given at the SS. Apostoli in that year; and composers usually superintended the production of their operas.

Cesti (born in Arezzo, or Florence, about 1620,
died in Venice in 1669), came to Venice, bringing the new Carissimi ideas, the new Carissimi
technique with him. Cesti brought the Opera
under the Carissimi influence ; and opera-composers, even Cavalli himself, were only too
amenable to it. As a purely musical influence,
it was nothing but good ; as a musico-dramatic
influence, it was unspeakably bad. Not only
did Cesti bring into Opera a number of highly-
developed musical forms of absolutely unscenic
character,—forms developed without a thought
of scenic requirements, and utterly unfit for
scenic uses,—but he turned the popular comic
element out of doors, and brought the Opera
back to its original estate of a form of art that
appealed well-nigh exclusively to a cultivated
aristocracy. With him came the severing of
the *opera buffa* from the *opera seria*. With him,
too, began the real dramatic decline of the latter form, a decadence more intrinsic and of
serious import than the mere change from
Tragedy to Melodrama in the earlier part of
the Venetian period. More to be lamented,
because, in a form of art which is (or ought to
be) nothing if not dramatic, a move in a poor
dramatic direction is far less ruinous than a
move in a distinctly undramatic direction. In
a word, coming under the Carissimi influence

did more harm to the Opera than anything else that ever happened to it; it led it into a no-thoroughfare from which no one succeeded in extricating it until Richard Wagner took the business in hand.

The *opera buffa* was far less amenable to this influence than the *opera seria ;* this was natural enough. But the *opera seria* was not long in contracting every undramatic and unscenic vice that has marred it, as a form of art, almost to this day. Opera entered upon what may well be called its "Oratorio epoch," becoming nothing but Oratorio sung in costume, amid more or less appropriate scenery.* This epoch had best be passed over by us here in silence, as the black, shameful period in the history of Opera. Enough that the Oratorio style of Italian *opera seria* flourished all through the so-called "great" Neapolitan period—roughly speaking, from 1684 to 1762 †—up to the Gluck Reform, that is, through the Handel period, in which it culminated. It was illustrated by some of the grandest and most exquisite music

---

* The term *Oratorio* is here used in its Handelian sense : as denoting a large form of vocal composition, not necessarily sacred, but of more or less dramatic character, intended for concert performance.

† These are the dates of the production in Naples of Alessandro Scarlatti's *Pompeo,* and of Gluck's *Orfeo ed Euridice* in Vienna.

ever written; nothing can exceed the beauty
of many things, for instance, in Handel's
operas.* But this music, though often essentially dramatic in its expression, was so antagonistic to all true scenic conditions that the
Opera of this epoch hardly deserves to be
ranked as Lyric Drama at all. The Lyric
Drama was virtually dethroned in this inter-
regnum of Oratorio.

One of the worst features of the business was
that it played into the hand of the virtuoso
singer as that worthy had never had it played
into before—even though Peri did condone the
Archilei's "*giri e gruppi*" in the very beginning.
Skilled singers knew well on which side their
bread was buttered, and the opportunity to
warble forth intoxicating roulades, without the
accompanying fatigue of acting, was not to be
despised; the whole epoch was their Golden
Age and happy hay-making time. The vocal
virtuoso soon got to be cock of the walk, and
composers themselves bowed down before him;
now and then, to be sure, a grandee like Handel
would try to throw a female of the species

---

* No adequate estimate of the greatness of George Frideric
Handel's genius can be formed from his oratorios; great as
these are in their way, they fall behind his Italian operas for
freshness of inspiration, originality of style, and poetic beauty of
conception.

bodily out of window, but such recalcitration was, upon the whole, rare. Not that the movement passed wholly without opposition. Matters had even come to a baddish pass before it got under way. Benedetto Marcello (1686–1739) gave up the whole business as a bad job after two or three trials, turned his back upon the stage for good and all, and betook himself to Church Music and Consuelo's "*I cieli immensi narranno*." Niccolò Jommelli (1714–1774) threw over the *da capo* aria, and made his music as dramatic as the less unscenic forms of the day would permit. But the singers had the best of it, and, where a man like Handel was willing to accept the general convention, the barking of smaller dogs went unheeded by the crowd. It was a deplorable business, and Gluck came not a day too soon, to put an end to it.

Meanwhile the comic form was faring better. It had long led a rather disreputable and unrecognized existence in many parts of Italy, haunting very minor theatres and other resorts of the proletariat; from popular it became plebeian. But, after a while, it began to show its face in good society again. At first in a small way, in the shape of one-act farces, often written by the singers themselves, given between the acts of grander operas; thus did it worm its way into court theatres, and sun itself once more in aristocratic smiles. Then came Niccolò Logroscino (born in Naples about 1700, died there in 1763) to make a reputable artistic form of it and get it recognized as a national institution. Pergolesi (1710–1736) and Piccinni (1728–1800) carried the form still farther upward in the artistic direction; the *opera buffa* was an established fact. Pergolesi's *Serva padrona* (Naples, 1731) long stood as the recognized *ne plus ultra* of the genre.

In Germany the Opera first made its appearance as an imported article of court luxury. The country was still down with the next-day's headache after its Thirty Years' War carouse, and princes and princekins had come to the conclusion that their most comfortable method of playing Saviour of Society would obviously be for each one to set up what best duodecimo Versailles of his own he could raise (on post-obit), and so put Hebrew cash to a Most Christian use. As anything wearing rouge was among the desirable appurtenances of such miniature Versailles, the Opera could not be unwelcome.

Quasi-operatic entertainments, of the Italian madrigal-play or even of the *vaudeville* sort, given by imported Italians, were not unknown. Duke Albrecht V gave one in Munich, for his son's nuptials, as early as 1568; and his example was imitated more than once in other parts of Germany. The first real opera given on German soil was also a direct imitation of the Italian model. Heinrich Schütz (1585–1672) was commissioned by Elector Johann Georg II, of Saxony, to write music to Rinuccini's libretto of *Dafne*, the German translator, Martin Opitz, not having succeeded in making his translation fit Peri's; this hybrid work was given in Dresden in 1627 (some say, in 1628). Though the score has been lost, there can be no doubt that the music was in the *stile rappresentativo* of the *Camerata;* Schütz had studied in Venice under Giovanni Gabrieli, but evidently found time to poke his nose into a good deal of the new Florentine and Mantuan music on the sly (his master not being disposed to favour that sort of thing), for his known compositions show the new influence. The earliest lyric drama of entirely Teutonic workmanship came seventeen years later, at Nuremberg in 1644; this was of an edifying, quasi-sacred character: *Das geistliche Waldgedicht oder Freudenspiel, genannt Seelewig*, by Sigismund Gottlieb Staden, organist at the Sebalduskirche (1607–1655). But here, too, one finds an unconcealed spirit of Italian imitation.

With *Daphne* and *Seelewig* German musical production for the stage seems to have gasped itself out for a while. With the middle of the century, Germany was thrown open to an Italian invasion; reigning sovereigns and rich nobles imported only Italian operas, with Italian companies to sing them. Cavalli comes to Vienna in 1658 to conduct his *Alessandro il grande, vincitor di se stesso;* Marchiati, Bernabei, Steffani, and a host of others flock to transalpine pastures, to fatten on German praise and pudding.

In 1678 the "first established German opera-house" was opened in Hamburg for the giving of operas in the German tongue. *Der erschaffene, gefallene und aufgerichtete Mensch,* otherwise known as *Adam und Eva,* was given on the opening night; a farrago of pseudo-philosophic Sunday-school religiosity, tempered with ballet-dancing, quite as astonishing as its title; the text by one Richter (who seems to have been a sort of Holy Roman Empire laureate in his way), the music by Johann Theile (1646–1724; pupil of Schütz, and teacher of Zachau, Hasse, and Buxtehude). Works like this, and also secular ones, written by Nikolaus Adam Strungk (1640–1700), Johann Wolfgang Franck (1641–1688), and Johann Philipp Förtsch (1652–1708), formed the staple of the repertory for some years. The libretti were, for the most part, villainous adaptations of Italian or French texts; the music, written in the clumsiest Italianizing vein.

But a change was not far off. In 1697 Reinhardt Keiser (1674-1739) came from the court of Braunschweig-Wolfenbüttel to settle in Hamburg; from that year, when his *Irene* was brought out, to 1734, the year of his *Circe*, his name was identified with the fortunes of the opera-house. Keiser stands in history as the great characteristic protagonist of German Opera in the first half of the eighteenth century. He gave up the Italianizing style of his predecessors, and wrote music that was essentially German in style and feeling. Unfortunately, his formula was none other than the Italian "Oratorio-Opera" formula of Scarlatti, Handel, and others of the Neapolitan school. So in Germany, too, do we find the trail of the Oratorio serpent over Opera, quite as much as in Italy.* Let Keiser's operas (well over a hundred of them, though the exact number is not known) remain in oblivion with Scarlatti's and Handel's.

In one respect, the Opera met with much the same fortunes in Hamburg that it did in Venice, a century earlier. The Hamburg movement,

---

* Let not this be deemed disrespectful to the (sometimes) sacred character of Oratorio. The serpent is mentioned in Holy Writ, and is, to that extent, a "sacred" animal.

like the Venetian before it, was intrinsically a
popular one : it meant Opera in the vernacular
for the people; and the comic element was
taken largely into account, even in some of the
earlier biblical works. Many of Förtsch's
operas were actual *Singspiele* (with spoken dialogue, like the French *opéra-comique*). But, with
Keiser's advent,—as with Cesti's in Venice,
—the aristocratic *opera seria*, of Oratorio cut,
began more and more to oust the popular form,
and soon reigned alone. Neither did this form
flourish in the vernacular long after Keiser's
death ; the Italian invasion swept over all Germany, and even native composers wrote to
Italian texts. Up to Mozart, the only national
form was the *Singspiel*,* which had been so well
killed by Keiser that it had to be virtually born
again, by imitating not very good French *opéras-
comiques* and still poorer English musical farces.
It did not attain to anything like maturity till
the time of Josef Haydn (1732–1809).

Upon the whole, the chief obstacle in the way
of the establishment and maintenance of a national form of Opera in Germany was a general
lack of innate dramatic sense in the people ; their
musical sense was fully as keen as that of the
Italians, but their dramatic sense was weak and

* Such of Gluck's serious operas as were given in German in
Vienna, and elsewhere, were first written for Paris in French.

easily satisfied. In France it was just the other way : there the obstacle was the combination of a very highly developed and fastidious dramatic sense with a merely rudimentary, but equally fastidious, musical sense. Where the Germans were ready to welcome Italian Opera with open arms, no matter how absurd the text and the relation of the music thereto, the French not only turned up their critical noses at the libretti offered them, but rejected much of the Italian music as beyond their comprehension.* They were disposed to be great sticklers for dramatic and scenic truth in the music of the Lyric Drama ; but, as none but the very simplest musical forms appealed to them, they could see scenic appositeness in these only.

Save for what have been called premonitory symptoms, of much the same sort as those already noted in Italy, the introduction of Opera into France, as into Germany, was owing to Italian influence. In 1645 a company of Italian players gave the *Festa teatrale della Finta pazza* before the queen at the palais du Petit-Bourbon : a five-act comedy with songs and decla-

---

* Not that they admitted this ; like other half-musical people, they were rich in plausible-sounding criticism on the " unnatural " exuberance of passion and the too extensive developments of Italian music. But the truth was that they had neither technical understanding of, nor temperamental sympathy with, it.

mation, not to mention dances of bears and monkeys, drinking ostriches, and other menagerie items. In 1646 cardinal Alessandro Bichi, bishop of Carpentras and apostolic nuncio of Urban VIII, gave a musical tragedy in the hall of his episcopal palace: *Achébar, roi du Mogol*, text and music by his secretary, the abbé Mailly. In 1647 cardinal Mazarin gave, at the Palais-Royal in Paris, a scenically sumptuous performance of an *Orfeo* by Luigi Rossi. Other Italian and one or two French ventures followed; among the latter, the *Pastorale en musique*, or *Opéra d'Issy*, of Lully and Cambert, in 1659, given (on Italian instigation) in private, and considered at the time to be quite in the Florentine *Camerata* vein. It was, however, only a quasi-dramatic cantata, not an opera ; but so successful that it had to be repeated in public. People began to talk of a "national" French form of Opera, fit to hold its own, and more, against anything of Italian importation. So wide awake had French chauvinism become that Cavalli (invited to Paris by Mazarin) made two downright fiascos—with his *Serse* in 1660, and his *Ercole amante* in 1662.

Shortly after the accession of Louis XIV to the throne, Pierre Perrin (1620–1675) obtained letters patent from the king (dated June 28, 1669) to establish an Academy of Music "like

those in Italy " for twelve years. He associated
with himself Robert Cambert (1628–1677), for
the music, the marquis de Sourdéac, for the
scenery and machines, and Bersac de Champeron, for the financial part ; a company was
formed, and, on March 19, 1671, the Académie
Royale de Musique was opened with *Pomone*,
a pastoral in a prologue and five acts, the text
by Perrin, the music by Cambert. Few institutions destined to exert a potent influence
over the world of Art have had so poor a beginning ; *Pomone* was about equally wretched
dramatically and musically. But it broke the
ice : the world-famous Académie de Musique
was a realized fact. It first occupied the jeu
de paume (tennis-court) de la Bouteille in the
rue des Fossés-de-Nesle (now rue Mazarine)
in the faubourg Saint-Germain.*

---

* It will be not uninteresting to give here at least five of the
thirteen houses successively occupied by this institution, and the
principal composers associated with each. The *premier Théâtre
du Palais-Royal* in the rue Saint-Honoré, between the rue de
Valois and the rue des Bons-Enfans (1673–1763, Lully-Rameau
period) ; the *deuxième Théâtre du Palais-Royal*, on the site of
the foregoing (1770–1781, Gluck-Piccinni period) ; the *Théâtre de
la République et des Arts* in the rue de la Loi, now rue de Richelieu (1794–1820, Spontini period) ; the *Salle provisoire* in the rue
Lepelletier (1821–1873, Auber-Rossini-Meyerbeer period, covering also the earlier years of Gounod) ; the present house in the
place de l'Opéra (1875). All but the last were burnt.

" *Dramatic truth of expression*."

If Perrin and Cambert were its founders, they can hardly be called the true founders of French Opera. This glory belongs to the Italian, Lully.

Giovanni Battista Lulli (Jean-Baptiste Lully after his naturalization in 1661) was born in Florence in 1633, and was taken by the chevalier de Guise to Paris, where he entered the service of mademoiselle de Montpensier as scullion. One day the comte de Nogent was attracted by his violin-playing, and he was promoted to a place among mademoiselle's musicians. Other promotions followed in time, with intermediate study of music under Metru, Roberdet, and Gigault, organists at Saint-Nicolas-des-Champs: positions at court, inspectorship of the "*grande bande*," conductorship of the "*petits violons*," posts of *surintendant de la musique de chambre, maître de musique* to the royal family, commissions to write ballets and divertissements for court festivities, even for Cavalli's operas. By intriguing with madame de Montespan he succeeded in jockeying Perrin and his associates out of their Académie de Musique *concession* in 1672 and having the direction transferred to himself. For the next fourteen years he displayed incomparable genius, talent, and business ability as composer, director, ballet-master, machinist, conductor, and even teacher of singers and dancers. A man of complete unscrupulousness and rascality, he managed to make himself indispensable, and held his post in spite of all opposition, not to mention a sense of impudent humour quite out of keeping with a courtier's prudence.*

After writing upwards of thirty ballets and divertissements (from 1658 to 1671, Molière's *Psyché* was the last) and twenty operas (1672–1686), beside no little instrumental and church music, this indefatigable "*coquin ténébreux*" (as Boileau called him) died in Paris on March 22, 1687—of an abscess in the foot, brought on by accidentally hitting his toe with his bâton while conducting.

In establishing the form known as French Grand Opera, Lully had the advantage of the collaboration of the dramatic poet Philippe Quinault, the author of most of his libretti. His task was none of the easiest : to adapt what was essentially Italian Opera to the French taste ; with Quinault's aid, he performed it, not only

---

* Once, when some trouble with the scenery delayed the raising of the curtain, word was brought him that the king was tired of waiting, and wished the performance to begin; "The king is master here," replied Lully like a shot, "*le roi est bien le maître*, and is free to be as tired of waiting as he pleases !" One can fancy the Grand Monarque's face when this was benevolently reported to him—as it undoubtedly was, for Lully did not lack "kind friends."

LULLY.

with genius, but with surpassing cleverness and insight into the French character. He had the wit to let his Italian musical instinct be guided by those principles of the Drama on which the French have ever prided themselves, as the first dramaturgic nation of the world. Musically his operas show the influence of Cavalli and other contemporary Venetians, which influence was already tinged by that of Carissimi and Cesti. But, in accepting the musical forms of Italian Opera,—not blindly, as Keiser did in Hamburg,—he wisely modified them in a way to make them appeal to the keen Gallic sense for dramatic fitness. He retained all that a half-musical, but dramatically fastidious, audience could understand,—among other things, the chorus, which the Venetians had banished, — but eliminated everything that would have been thrown away upon his particular public. His style is marked by great musical simplicity and a poignant truthfulness of dramatic expression; his music seldom lacks a distinctly scenic quality, it is eminently fitted for the stage.*

---

* Regarding this matter, it should be remembered that the scenic requirements of the classic French *tragédie*—to which class of Drama Lully's libretti for the most part belonged—were not very great. There was more haranguing than dramatic action, in the Shaksperian sense.

The form of serious Opera established by Lully long remained the standard norm in France. What subsequent modifications it underwent—at the hands of Gluck and others—were more of the nature of natural progressive developments than of radical changes. Lully's works held the stage unrivalled, for he had no worthy immediate French successors, until the advent of Jean-Philippe Rameau (born at Dijon in 1683, died in Paris in 1764).

Rameau was a far abler technical musician than Lully; his fame as a musical theorist, as the first founder of a System of Harmony, need only be alluded to here. Indeed, so great was he as organist, clavecinist, and writer for those instruments, that nothing save the predestination of his Gallic blood can explain his ever taking up Opera at all. As it was, he only began to write for the stage in his fiftieth year.

As a dramatic composer, Rameau compares with Lully very much as Cavalli does with Monteverdi. Both Monteverdi and Lully threw their whole weight upon dramatic truth of expression, as a matter of well-grounded artistic principle; they were consequently exceedingly fastidious about the character and quality of their libretti. Cavalli and Rameau cared not a whit what they set to music, and were dramatic more by unconquerable instinct than by

48

calculation. The influence they exerted upon the evolution of the Opera tended more in a musical than in a dramatic direction. And yet, such is the mysterious nature of the Art of Tones, one can not say that the results they achieved were less intrinsically dramatic than those obtained by Monteverdi and Lully, in spite of a certain evident inconsistency in the means employed. Rameau's *Hippolyte et Aricie* (1733), *Dardanus* (1739), and a few other operas held the stage well into the Gluck period. He closed what may be called the first epoch of French Grand Opera, a form of Opera which, notwithstanding a certain rigid conventionality of style, never descended to the unscenic absurdities of the Italian " Oratorio " type. Side by side with it, however, the imported Italian article—sung by Italians in Italian—flourished more and more in France. The old chauvinism which had crushed Cavalli in 1660 gradually lost its grip, and, considerably before the rivalry between the two great champions, Gluck and Piccinni, the French opera-going public was split up into two opposing parties : the Italophiles and the Nationalists. The Italian conquest swept over France, too, but not, as in Germany, to even a temporary extinction of native Opera.

It has often been stated that the Opera was

developed in England from the Masque; but
this is only partly true. As a gorgeous piece
of poetic stage pageantry with incidental music,
the Masque evidently needed but a magical
touch—like Baltazarini's in the *Ballet de la
Reine*, giving more dramatic consistency to the
scheme—to turn it into something quite as like
Opera as the French court ballet of 1581. The
nearer the Masque approached the real Drama,
the nearer would it, almost *propter hoc*, approach the Opera. In 1617 Nicolo Laniere
(born in London, of Italian parents, about 1590,
died between 1665 and 1670) set the whole text
of the masque by Ben Jonson that was given
at Lord Hay's house to music in the "*stile
recitativo*" (clearly enough, the *stile rappresentativo* of the *Camerata*). This is the earliest
known instance of the whole of a dramatic, or
quasi-dramatic, text being set to music in England; the model upon which it was evidently
based, the original Florentine *favola in musica*,
was then twenty years old. But this first attempt, like the French *Ballet de la Reine*, was a
mere flash in the pan; it found no imitators,
and the music of the Masque fell back into its
original incidental estate.

A more germane source of the Opera in England is to be found in the long-familiar incidental music in the spoken Drama. This was

developed by one man into something more closely resembling Opera than anything else known in the country before the Italian invasion of the first quarter of the eighteenth century—on one occasion, into Opera itself. This man was Henry Purcell (born in London about 1658, died there on November 21, 1695), the last genius of the first rank England ever gave to the Art of Music. Purcell studied composition under Pelham Humphries, who was a pupil of Lully's, and no doubt studied some of the French master's scores, possibly also one or two of Cavalli's, with considerable assiduity. He wrote music to masques and plays, some of which latter were even called operas on the title-page. But only one really was an opera.* Beside what is commonly known as incidental music,—overtures, interludes, and such instrumental and vocal music as is indicated in the author's stage-directions,—Purcell would at times set the text of a scene, or part of a scene, quite in the operatic way. Such scenes thus became actual operatic fragments; Purcell's setting of

* The line of demarcation between a play with incidental music and an opera, like that between *opéra-comique* and *vaudeville*, must be drawn somewhere. The small proportion of the music to the text, also the fact that the play begins as a spoken drama, the music only coming in later, should be enough to put all but one of Purcell's dramatic works out of the operatic category.

them, not to mention the genius displayed, was so far in advance of anything of the sort known in any part of Europe in his day, in point of dramatic and musical freedom and scenic quality, that one can only regret his early death's preventing his taking to opera-writing on a larger scale. Leaving intrinsic genius out of the question,—which would be largely on Purcell's side,—some of his musical scenes come quite up to anything by Gluck; the musical treatment is at once as free, as unhampered by convention, as essentially dramatic and scenic. Purcell wrote music to some forty and odd plays, the first being Nahum Tate's *Dido and Æneas* (1675),* and the last, *Bonduca*, altered from Beaumont and Fletcher (given posthumously in 1696).

He had no worthy successor; indeed, the decline of English Music may be said to have begun with his death. When George Frideric Handel (1685–1759) came to London, and his *Rinaldo* was brought out there in 1711, England was in just the condition to become the easiest sort of prey to the Italian invasion. In 1720 came Giovanni Battista Bononcini (1660–1750), in 1721, Attilio Ariosti (1660– ?), and Italian

---

* This was his only real opera. The brevity of the text, if nothing else, shows that the whole libretto was written especially for musical setting.

Opera of the most pronounced "Oratorio" type had the whole field to itself. In Handel we descry the culmination of the fatal Carissimi influence upon the Opera; with him the "Oratorio" type attained to its fullest bloom—in perfection of plastic and imaginative musical beauty, in utter dearth of scenic quality.

But, though Italian Opera reigned for a while alone in England, it did not reign unopposed; the English could not but feel the inherent absurdity of the form. In 1728 John Rich brought out at his theatre in Lincoln's Inn Fields *The Beggar's Opera*, the text by John Gay, the music arranged from popular ballads by Dr. Pepusch (born in Berlin in 1667, died in London in 1752). This was the beginning of the English Ballad Opera, the only form the English have since cultivated with success.* Charles Dibdin's (1745–1814) operas, even the Gilbert and Sullivan operettas of our own day, all come from this stock.

Thus did the Opera make the conquest of Europe; the Italian form carrying out a successful invasion, and native forms springing up in imitation of it, in France, Germany, and England.

---

* Unless we except the operas of Michael William Balfe (1808–1870) and Vincent Wallace (1814–1865), which stagger about rather uncertainly between the Italian *opera seria* and the native Ballad model.

III

Gluck

IN the year 1741, when Handel's last opera, *Deidamia*, was given in London, Gluck's first, *Artaserse*, was brought out in Milan ; a coincidence to be deemed significant by the superstitious. The grand autocrat of the old régime makes his parting bow just as the herald of the new comes upon the scene ; *le Roy est mort ! vive le Roy !*

Christoph Willibald Gluck—afterward fond of insisting upon his title of Ritter von Gluck (he was made *cavaliere* of the Order of the *Sprone d'Oro* in Rome in 1754)—was born at the village of Weidenwang, near Neumarkt in the Upper Palatinate, on July 2, 1714. His parents were in the service of Prinz Lobkowitz, and he passed his childhood at the prince's castle of Eisenberg. His education was tolerably well cared for, according to the notions of the day ; at twelve he was sent to a Jesuit school at Kommotau in Bohemia ; at eighteen, to Prag, where he studied music under Bohuslav Černohorský, and took to practising on the 'cello. In 1736, being then twenty-two, he entered the private band of prince Melzi in Vienna, soon following his patron to Milan, where he finished his professional studies under Sammartini.* After four years' work at counterpoint and other forms of composition, he felt himself ready to face the world as a composer "*en gros*," as Mendelssohn would have said. †

He had rare good luck: some things he had written for prince Melzi's chamber-music got him the commission to write a grand opera for the court theatre. For his libretto he took Metastasio's *Artaserse*. Even in this, his first opera, he determined to cut loose from many of the traditions of the "Oratorio" school, and write music that should be at once more dramatic and more scenic. But he told no one of his intention, and finished his score—all but one aria—to suit himself. With this one aria lacking, the opera was put into rehearsal, and every musical dabster present pooh-poohed the "new style" most contemptuously. This Gluck had counted on; before the final rehearsal he wrote

[handwritten margin note: the Court poet, of prince Melzi in Vienna]

[handwritten margin note: In Scala 1741]

---

* Giovanni Battista Sammartini, who ran a good third to the tie between Boccherini and Josef Haydn in the legendary race for the "invention" of the string quartet.

† "I am a wholesale pianist (*engros Pianist*); I can't play small things in public!"—FELIX MENDELSSOHN, *reported orally*.

the missing aria wholly in the conventional style, and a still larger gathering of *cognoscenti* than had been at the first rehearsal praised it highly, even suspecting it of coming from the pen of Sammartini himself. The audience on the opening night straightway quashed this verdict, though, crying out that that particular aria was simply insipid and quite unworthy of the rest of the score. Thus did our young Oberpfälzer slyboots score one off his first judges!

So Gluck had from the first this ambition to make the Opera more dramatic than his predecessors and contemporaries had done. But he had as yet no definite formula; his innovations were still evolutionary, rather than revolutionary; he did nothing that could be called radical. Yet what he did was new enough to scare the critics, who, as academic policemen, guarded nothing more carefully than the inviolable sacredness of traditional forms. But, if severely handled at times by the critics, Gluck would now and then get compensating sympathy from others. When a certain passage in the aria "*Se mai senti spirarti sul volto*," in his *Clemenza di Tito* (Naples, 1751), was scathingly criticised, it was shown to old Durante,* who

---

* Francesco Durante (1684–1755), then, at the age of sixty-seven, the recognized supreme master of Neapolitan church music.

said : "I do not feel like deciding whether this passage is entirely in accordance with the rules of composition ; but this I can tell you, that all of us, myself to begin with, would be very proud of having thought of and written such a passage !"

From 1741 on, Gluck continued writing Italian operas; with enormous success in Italy and Vienna, in spite of the critics, if with no success whatever in England. He travelled a good deal, and the hearing of some Rameau operas in Paris must have given him wholesome food for meditation. From about 1755 to 1761 he showed signs of lapsing into mere conventionalism, and seemed to treat opera-writing as sheer practice-work, to gain technical facility. His mind was really filled with other matters ; he had been for some time applying himself with zeal to filling out the gaps in his defective general education, studying æsthetics, languages, and literature, and getting what good he could from frequenting the society of cultivated people. He had plainly become dissatisfied with the scope and efficacy of his dramatic innovations in Opera, and was meditating a more thorough and logically formulated reform.

At last (about 1760) he met the right man to help him : the Italian poet Raniero de' Calzabigi, of Leghorn, editor of Metastasio's works in Paris, Counsellor at the Netherland Chamber of Accounts in Vienna, noted writer on æsthetics, etc., etc. With him he talked the problem over: the defects of the Italian *opera seria*, and how these defects were best to be cured. The two pitched upon the following items as lying at the root of the reigning evil: the irresponsible vanity of the virtuoso singer, and the flaccid conventionality of the Metastasio libretto—full of poetic beauty (of a sort), but almost totally lacking dramatic quality, especially such as could be intensified by music.

The practical upshot was that Calzabigi wrote the text of *Orfeo ed Euridice*, and Gluck set it to music. One can not help smiling at the work's having first to be submitted to Metastasio, to avoid the foregone conclusion of a fiasco; the court poet's influence was not to be trifled with! Still more must one smile at Metastasio's carrying his friendship for Gluck and Calzabigi to the point of "agreeing to offer no active opposition to the new work," sure in his good heart that the public would take the trouble of damning it off his hands; he little dreamt that he was digging his own grave!

Orfeo, brought out at the Vienna Burgtheater on October 5, 1762, was the first cannon-shot of the new Revolution. It was no "*Veni, vidi, vici,*" being considerably discussed at first; but the public came to it gradually, and Gluck's campaign opened with a very palpable victory. Much the same was true of *Alceste*—the libretto by Calzabigi, after Euripides—given on December 26, 1766. This work fairly separated the sheep from the goats in the Viennese public; the more seriously inclined saw that it was on a still higher plane of tragic grandeur than *Orfeo*, but a large mass of opera-goers found it rather too much of a good thing. "If that is the sort of evening's entertainment the Court Opera is to provide, good bye; we can go to church without paying two Gulden!" Gluck had to find out that fighting long-established convention is no bed of roses, and that impeccably attired patrons of aristocratic Opera are much inclined to resent seriousness that has not been cured of its deformity by sweetly-warbling divinities of the virtuoso species. But unquestionable success came with time, and *Alceste* established Gluck's position even more firmly than *Orfeo* had done.

Passing over *Paride ed Elena*—a strong work, but ill received by the public—and some other minor matters, we come to Gluck's meeting with the second poet who was to have a determining influence upon his destiny: the bailli du Rollet, attaché to the French legation in Vienna. Du Rollet encouraged Gluck's already-formed wish to go to Paris, as the properest field for him. He had become dissatisfied with the executive means he found in Vienna, and longed for the Académie de Musique, where there were "well skilled and intelligent actors, who combined a noble and soulful play of gesture with the art of song." Du Rollet took Racine's *Iphigénie en Aulide* and turned it into a libretto, Gluck setting to work forthwith upon the score; even before it was completed, it was pronounced to be just the thing for Paris.

To wish to go to Paris was one thing; to get officially invited thither, another. It seemed to French chauvinism that Paris had already quite foreigners enough to put up with in resident Italian musicians, and that the prospect of having to do with an admittedly strong German, and an æsthetic revolutionary to boot, was rather appalling. There was plotting and counterplotting galore, letter-writing without end. At last Marie Antoinette's influence carried the day,—she had been Gluck's pupil in Vienna, before her marriage,—and she succeeded in doing more for her former teacher than crowned heads or rich patrons (who have troubles of their own) often do for those who need their help. But Marie Antoinette's getting Gluck his invitation was enough to set madame Dubarry tooth and nail against him—

GLUCK.

just to show the world that a king's particular
Fair Perdition was not to be outdone in court
influence by any woman alive, let alone a Dau-
phine! The Dubarry was really at the bottom
of most of the anti-Gluck agitation in Paris.

When Gluck came to Paris in 1773, with his
Iphigénie all ready for the boards, his expecta-
tions of the *personnel* of the Académie de Musique were not wholly fulfilled. He found the
acting as good as he had expected, but princi-
pals, chorus, and orchestra had fallen into the
most deplorable musical habits; it took all his
personal force, indomitable Teutonic pertina-
city, and skill as a conductor, to whip them up to
the mark. He succeeded, though, and *Iphigénie en Aulide* was brought to a satisfactory performance on April 19, 1774. It made a colder
impression at first than any of his operas had
in Vienna, but, like them, gradually made its
way with the public. Then the storm broke
loose!

The chief contestants in this famous Gluck
controversy were, on Gluck's side, the abbé
Arnaud and the "*Anonyme de Vaugirard*" (really
Suard by name); on the opposing side, Marmontel, La Harpe, Guinguené, d'Alembert, the
chevalier de Chastilleux, Framéry, and Co-
queau. Grimm held a dignifiedly neutral position, or tried to make believe he did; two of

the most important of Gluck's favourers were Jean-Jacques and Voltaire, but neither of the two took any active part in the fight. La Harpe—whose sharp wit fairly took the bit in its teeth, and got beyond his own or any one's control—was the *enfant terrible* of the whole business, and did his own side as much harm as good; the Anonyme de Vaugirard took an especial delight in getting a rise out of him and prodding him to desperation.

Upon the whole, with all the wit, acute thought, and literary ability brought to bear upon the matter, first and last, this once-great controversy is no very edifying reading now; what controversialists on new æsthetic problems most lack is originality, the new problems suggest to them no new arguments, neither does the world's past experience in similar cases stead them a jot. It is always the same old story, over and over again, this organized kicking against the Rising Sun. Read the discussion between Monteverdi and Artusi in the first decade of the seventeenth century, the pen-and-ink tiffs between Wagnerians and anti-Wagnerians in the third quarter of the nineteenth, and you will have read practically all that was urged for and against Gluck in Paris in the 'seventies of the eighteenth. It was, in the last analysis, merely a Wotan and Fricka

business,* a volcanic conspuation of the New,
"*des Niedagewesenen,*" on the one hand, a firmly
convinced championing of it, on the other. The
anti-Gluck side of the controversy is well sum-
marized by Schmid: † "These criticisms had
two different purposes: first, they tried to prove
that the Ritter von Gluck lacked all power of
song, and next, that he set things to music that
were not appropriate to song." And, if the intelligent reader knows of any "new light" in
the whole history of Lyric Drama of whom
this has not been said, he will confer a favour
upon the present author by mentioning his
name!

The impression produced by *Iphigénie en
Aulide* as the performances wore on was still
strengthened by *Orphée et Euridice*, given in
August, 1774, in a translation by Moline, with
the part of Orphée, originally written for con-

---

* FRICKA

Wann—ward es erlebt,
dass, etc.?

WOTAN

Heut'—hast du's erlebt!
WAGNER, *Die Walküre*, Act II., Scene I.

(*Fricka*—Who ever lived to see that, etc.? *Wotan*—To-day hast
thou lived to see it!)

† ANTON SCHMID, *Christoph Willibald, Ritter von Gluck*, page
277. Leipzig: Friedrich Fleischer, 1854.

tralto, transposed for Legros's high tenor. Of
l'Arbre enchanté (Versailles, February 20, 1775)
and the three-act ballet *Cythère assiégée* (Académie de Musique, August 1, 1775), nothing need
be said here. Gluck had returned to Vienna
for a while, taking with him a remodelled version of the text of his *Alceste* by du Rollet and
Quinault's libretto of *Armide et Renaud*, meaning to retouch the former score, and reset the
latter text, for Paris. He was at work on both
scores in Vienna when he got news of the
latest trick of his opponents in Paris: the Italian, Piccinni, had been invited, and was to set
Quinault's *Roland* for the Académie de Musique.
Gluck's pride was bitten to the quick; a flaming
letter of his to du Rollet found its way (without
his leave) into the *Année littéraire*, and only
served still further to exasperate the opposition. The Italophiles now had a champion of
their own, and the Gluck controversy became
the Gluck-Piccinni war, compared to which the
old Handel-Bononcini business in London was
a mere squabble.

In 1776 Gluck came back to Paris, and *Alceste* was given at the Académie de Musique on
April 23. It was a bad night for the Gluckists;
the opera was roundly hissed, the disappointed
composer whimpering out " *Alceste est tombée !* "
upon a friend's shoulder. " *Oui, tombée du ciel !* "

replied the latter, fain to seek consolation in an epigram. But the fiasco was only for a while; *Alceste's* gradual success in Vienna was repeated in Paris, and Gluck once more ended by carrying the day.

On September 23, 1777, *Armide* was brought out; the immediate result was about the same as usual, only that indifference took the place of hissing. For one thing, the anti-Gluckists could not howl at Gluck's "impudence" in daring to reset a text already set by the great Lully, as it had been feared they would; for their own Piccinni had put them in a glass house by setting Quinault's *Roland*, of which Lully was also the original composer.* Moreover, Gluck had paid French taste no mean compliment in taking Quinault's *Armide et Renaud* exactly as it stood, without subjecting it to those modifications which he had had made in all his previous classical libretti. But the indifference with which *Armide* was greeted at first soon wore off, and by the time Piccinni was ready with his *Roland* Gluck's position was again very strong indeed. Piccinni, to say the truth, was rather a laggardly champion, taking an infinite time in coming up to the scratch; which is partly to be accounted for

---

* Piccinni did not, like Gluck, set Quinault's text as it stood, but in an adaptation by Marmontel.

by the poor man's not knowing a word of French when he first set to work upon his score. But on January 27, 1778, *Roland* was at last brought out, after endless trouble and squabbling at rehearsals; as a first cannon-shot into the Gluckist camp, it did a certain amount of execution, at least, the controversy became doubly acrid after it. It remained at white heat until the final "duel" settled matters.

It was agreed that both Gluck and Piccinni should write an opera, *Iphigénie en Tauride;* they could thus fight it out between them on the same ground. Gluck took a libretto by Guillard; Piccinni, one by Dubreuil. This "duel," as usual, was rather a long one, Gluck's opera being given on May 18, 1779, Piccinni's not till January 23, 1781 — some time after Gluck had left Paris for good. The result, however, was decisive; Gluck's *Iphigénie* capped the climax of his Paris successes, was indeed the first of his Paris operas that won unquestionable public favour on the opening night, whereas Piccinni's had a mere *succès d'estime* even with its own party, the more eager of whom tried to explain its quasi-failure with the general public by the undeniable fact that, on the second night, the beauteous Laguerre (who sang Iphigénie) was hopelessly the worse for strong liquor—"*Iphigénie en Champagne!*"

said pert Sophie Arnould, who had sung Gluck's first Iphigénie.

It is quite plain that the success of Gluck's *Iphigénie en Tauride* was thoroughly genuine, based on the quality of the work itself. No less strong an opera could have so utterly routed Piccinni's as it did; especially as Gluck, after his *Iphigénie*, had had a palpable failure with his *Écho et Narcisse* on September 24, 1779, thus leaving Paris with his latest opera on record as a fiasco. Piccinni was, in truth, no weakling at all; he was even something of a dramatic reformer in Opera himself, quite as much as Gluck in his earlier Italian and Viennese days. But Gluck had far outstripped him since then, and had, moreover, as much greater force of innate genius than he as Handel had than Bononcini. Piccinni was swept from the stage into oblivion, not because he was weak, but because Gluck was stronger; also because the Gluck idea was stouter and truer than his. Had he not been inadvisedly brought to Paris to take part in that unequal contest with the doughty Austrian, he might have gone comfortably down in history as a worthy forerunner of the Gluck Reform; but, being thus brought face to face with and in opposition to it, he was crushed.

Écho et Narcisse was Gluck's last work for

the stage; with it he leaves the history of Opera.* He died of apoplexy in Vienna on November 15, 1787.

As a reformer, Gluck was but little of a radical, hardly anything of a theorist. The best confession of artistic faith we have from his pen, his preface to *Alceste*,† stands in history, with Peri's to *Euridice* and Victor Hugo's to *Cromwell*, as one of the most famous of its kind. But there is very little constructive theorizing in it; it is, for the most part, negative in character, pointing out what is most to be avoided in opera-writing. It is a document of sheer sound artistic common sense, not a philosophico-scientific marshalling of principles to a firmly based theory; admirable as far as it goes, but not going far. Had Gluck's Reform rested with this document alone, there would have been little life in it.

The real essence and mainspring of this

---

* *Les Danaïdes* (text by du Rollet and Tschudi), which was brought out at the Académie de Musique on April 26, 1784, was advertised as "by Gluck and Salieri"; but, after the thirteenth performance, Gluck announced that the score was entirely by Salieri. The libretto was sent to Gluck in 1783, with the request to write the score; but he did not feel in condition to undertake the work then, and handed over the text to his pupil—"the foreigner who alone had learnt his manner of him, since no German cared to."

† *Vide* Appendix, page 227.

much-talked-of Reform was Gluck's own intrinsic dramatic genius; his true strength as a reformer lay in his work, not in his doctrine. In him the old dramatic spirit of Peri, Monteverdi, and Cavalli breathed fresh and strong again; and it was the vigourous expression he gave to this spirit in his music that won him adherents, while his ruthless sacrifice of the time-honoured conventional operatic frippery to this expression made him enemies among those to whom old habits were dear.

What was new in Gluck was his musico-dramatic individuality, his style; for there was little really new in his principles. Not only did these date back, as far as they went, to the earliest days of Opera, but the artistic sins and abuses he stigmatized—the slavish subserviency of composers to the whims of the virtuoso singer, the sacrifice of dramatic interest to irrelevant musical developments—had been pointed out and deplored by more than one musician before him.

Gluck's Reform did not lack precursory heralds; the evils he set himself to cure had long been recognized as such, and he was not the first to attempt to cure them. But he was the first to strike the decisive blow, to go, if not quite to the root of the matter, at least as near to the root as was necessary for his purpose.

And, as for his lack of radicalism, note how, in his preface, all even of the negative theses have their conditioning *if* or *when*. He does not oppose vocal ornamentation, for instance, absolutely and along the whole line, but only when it becomes damaging to dramatic common sense. He showed the same lack of uncompromising radicalism in his practice : there is many a vocal show-piece in his operas, but brought in in the right place, not into the midst of an ardent dramatic action.

Gluck is fairly to be regarded as the Father of Modern Opera; a sufficient commentary on this is the very fact that his are the earliest operas that hold the stage to this day. He followed Philipp Emanuel Bach and Haydn in employing a standard composition of the orchestra,* and banished the time-honoured *cembalo* (harpsichord) from it; he was thus the first opera-composer to write out his scores completely, leaving nothing to be added by the cembalist. He was equally great in impassioned or pathetic melody and in every form of recitative; his dramatic use of the chorus can hardly be surpassed in mastery. The opening scenes of the first and second acts of his *Orfeo*

---

* Up to, and including, Handel, there had been no standard composition of the orchestra, the aggregations of instruments used by composers being exceedingly various.

—Euridice's funeral rites, and Orfeo's entrance into Hades—are still unsurpassed masterpieces in this last particular.

Like most "new" men, Gluck was terribly fastidious about the style in which his works were to be given. Concerning Orfeo's aria, "*Che farò senza Euridice?*" he writes to the duke of Braganza:* "Were one to make the slightest change in it, in the tempo or the mode of expression, it would become an air for the marionette stage. In a piece of this order, a more or less sustained note, a forcing of the tone, a neglect of the proper tempo, a trill, roulade, etc., can entirely destroy the effect of a scene." He was an inexorable rehearser, infinitely hard to satisfy.

In a specific sense, Gluck's great achievement was to fix the form of French Grand Opera for nearly a century, taking the form as already established by Lully and Rameau for a basis. What may be called the Gluck formula subsisted with but slight modification in France until Meyerbeer came above the horizon. From *Orfeo ed Euridice* to *Iphigénie en Tauride*, his operas are distinctly *grand* operas ; to produce their proper effect, they need not only fine acting and singing and a competent orchestra, but a vast, well equipped stage and the most

---

* Preface to *Paride ed Elena*, 1770.

copious spectacular paraphernalia, especially a superb ballet. They are essentially spectacular operas, and it is the prominence of this feature in them that has most militated against their being adequately given in this country.

Gluck united in an unparalleled degree warmth of temperament with a certain classic reserve in expression; he was at home in classical and mythological subjects, in the stately classic manner; the true "romantic" strenuousness he had not, he would have made but a poor hand at it with a Shaksperian libretto. But it would be a dull ear that could not catch the poignancy that lurks behind his measured dignity of expression, a dull heart that did not beat responsively to the expansive force of his emotional heat. Perhaps he is at his most poignant in his musical pictures of perfect happiness; in grief and pathos he is great, but in serene, unalloyed bliss, greater still. There is a deeper well of tears in the chorus of beatified spirits in his *Orfeo*, than in "*Che farò senza Euridice?*" or "*Malheureuse Iphigénie!*" Few men have produced such overwhelming effects on the lyric stage with so beautiful a simplicity of means; let us part from him with his pet maxim (whether wholly true or not, matters little) on his lips: "Simplicity and Truth are the sole right principles of the Beautiful in works of art."

72

IV

Mozart

A SHARPER contrast than that between Gluck and Mozart—both of them men of surpassing genius, both great in very nearly the same line—can hardly be found in History, which, like melodrama, is rather rich in sharp contrasts. Gluck, warm and impulsive in feeling, was a thinker, a man of ideas, a born champion and espouser of causes; keen of perception and instinct, he was yet well persuaded of the need of weighing his perceptions intellectually and rationally, that his championship might be efficacious. Inconspicuous as the *Alceste* preface is as a documentary statement of art principles, one can not but see that it represents an immense amount of solid thinking. In short, Gluck was a man who could be truly great only by seconding his native genius with a complete intellectual grasp of the why and wherefore of the business in hand; and, having this grasp, he could claim entire responsibility for everything great he did.

Mozart was his direct antithesis, as irresponsible a person as can be found in the whole tale of opera-composers, Cavalli included. Gifted with vastly superior genius to Gluck's, he had in very truth nothing but this genius, and the unerring accuracy of immediate perception that went therewith. He was decidedly an ordinary man intellectually; outside of his music, without a single intellectual taste. Where Gluck, impelled by a burning sense of the deficiencies of his early education, studied literature and æsthetics, the whole literature, the whole æsthetic movement, of his day left Mozart absolutely untouched; were he alive to-day, he would read nothing but a newspaper. As a boy, he evinced a certain genial brightness of precocious wit and humour; his early letters may be accounted more than ordinarily good boy's letters. But this precocious intellectuality faded out of him with manhood; his later letters show a certain hard-and-fast common sense, but of a quite conventional sort.

What most makes Mozart remarkable is not so much the greatness as the unparalleled self-sufficiency (in a good sense) of his genius. By dint of sheer genius alone,—backed up, to be sure, by an exceptionally fine special, technical education; for old Leopold, his father, was the best of musical drill-masters,—he did what

74

hardly another man has done with commanding intellect, genius, and culture combined. To be sure, there must have been a profound intellectuality latent in him somewhere, for few men have written music which furnishes the listener and student with a greater wealth of food for thought. No intellectual problem, so to speak, was too high nor too deep for him to solve musically; but his unerring dive to the heart of every matter was guided by sheer instinct; he perceived immediately and intuitively what other men had to get at by hard thinking. Pure genius, nothing but genius and an unsurpassed technique, was all he had in his armoury; and with these weapons alone he showed himself fully up to the level of every emergency. His fellow is not to be found in the history of the Opera.

No bad commentary on the man's purely instinctive and unreflective bent is the fact that, with the example of Gluck and his Reform fresh before his very eyes, he went to work with his opera-writing as if Gluck had never existed; he utterly ignored the Gluck movement. It were wholly wrong to suppose that Mozart began where Gluck left off; he did nothing of the sort, he began where Gluck himself began, and went his own way. Gluck had a formula of his own; Mozart had (con-

sciously) none. Yet he raised the Lyric Drama
to a height it had never attained before, which
it has reached only once or twice since. For,
hazardous as is every comparison between
works of utterly different character, it is not
too much to say that only Wagner's *Tristan
und Isolde* and *Die Meistersinger* can rank with
Mozart's *Don Giovanni* as completely great
works of art; nothing else in all Lyric Drama
maintains itself throughout on quite so high a
plane—intellectually, musically, dramatically.

Mozart's life is not particularly interesting,
nor, save that he travelled a good deal, very
full of incident. He was born at Salzburg on
January 27, 1756, and christened Johannes Chry-
sostomus Wolfgangus Theophilus; for a while,
as a boy, he would add his confirmation name,
Sigismundus, in his signature; to history he has
ever been Wolfgang Amadeus (the latter being
the Latin for Theophilus). His father, Leopold
Mozart, was an excellent violinist and a thorough musician, especially great as a teacher.

Wolfgang's precocity and child-wonderhood
have been much dwelt upon; but, though certainly remarkable in this respect, he is neither
the only nor the most remarkable instance of
precocious genius on record.* True, he was

* Although Mozart had won a solid reputation as a composer
at thirteen, up to seventeen or eighteen he had produced nothing

76

MOZART.

only fifteen when his *Ascanio in Alba* eclipsed Hasse's *Ruggiero* in Milan; but the old *Sassone* was seventy-one at the time, and had outlived his best powers. Wolfgang and his sister Marianne lived the life of infant prodigies from 1762 to 1769, travelling much with their father, the boy doing quite as much composing as pianoforte- or violin-playing. He excited admiration everywhere, wrote his first opera, *La finta semplice*, in Vienna in 1768, was appointed Conzertmeister (without salary) to the Archbishop of Salzburg in 1769, and got the *Sprone a'Oro* ("the same as Gluck's") in Rome in 1770. Beside his father's teaching, he had studied also under Sammartini (Gluck's teacher) and the great Padre Martini; in fact, in a technical educational way, he had the very best advantages, as indeed he has ever been recognized as one of the most complete masters of musical technics, form, and style. The rest of his too short life was a hardly intermittent struggle with poverty and the coarse misappreciation of ill-paying patrons. On August 16, 1782, he married the singer Constanze Weber (first cousin of Karl Maria von Weber), after being jilted by her elder sister Aloysia. He died of malig-

fairly comparable, for maturity of ideas and style, to Mendelssohn's E-flat major octet (written at sixteen), or Richard Strauss's F minor symphony (written at seventeen).

nant typhus in Vienna on December 5, 1791. For him, who had been chivied and put upon by grandees for the better part of his life, an unrecognized pauper's grave was perhaps as fitting a *Requiescat* as another.

Mozart's position in the history of Opera is so unique that he can hardly be treated historically like other opera-composers. He founded no school, and left no imitators behind him; indeed, there was nothing imitable about him. As has been said, he raised the Lyric Drama to an unprecedented and since unsurpassed height by sheer force of genius, without apparently giving the matter any thought at all—certainly no original thought. It seems never to have entered his head that he might have a "mission"; he was in no sense a reformer, like Gluck. It is not unsignificant that almost the last libretto he set to music was by Metastasio! To be sure, he was no slavish follower of precedent, and wrote exactly as he pleased, often doing quite unprecedented things. The second finale of his *Don Giovanni* shows him with one foot thrust well over the wall of time into Beethoven's *Eroica*. But he evinced no set purpose to be off with the old or on with the new. Like Cavalli, he was by no means fastidious about his libretti, and took them pretty much as they came.

What he did bring to bear upon the operatic problem—little of a problem, though, to him! —was a wholly new individuality. Two new items he certainly did introduce into opera-writing. He was the first composer to strike unmistakably the "modern romantic" note in Opera; he revived the long-dead art of musical character-drawing. He did not create it, for there are some rather surprising instances of sharp musical delineation of character to be found in Monteverdi and Cavalli, especially in the latter; but the "Oratorio" school had pretty much done away with all that, and Mozart gave it due prominence again. Gluck can not compare with him in this matter; as a creator of "living figures of flesh and blood" in Lyric Drama, Mozart has never been surpassed, and equalled now and then only by Richard Wagner.

It is not a little remarkable that this power of Mozart's, of putting thoroughly real-seeming and strongly individualized people upon the lyric stage, should have gone hand in hand with an unconquerable, one had almost said, an excessive bent toward ideality. True as he was to the core, he absolutely could not help idealizing; *c'était plus fort que lui!* As Hanslick once said, the rascally little Cherubino in da Ponte's version of Caron de Beaumarchais's

Figaro turns into an actual cherub in his hands; the pert little village coquette, Zerlina, becomes absolutely angelic. Yet, such is the genius with which it is done, you accept it all readily; you would not have it otherwise.

Perhaps as characteristic an example as another of this inveterate ideality of Mozart's, and of the astonishing way he made it go hand in hand with dramatic truth, is the little quintet, "*Di scrivermi ogni giorno*" in *Così fan tutte*. The situation is purely ludicrous: two young officers, secretly on forbidden pleasure bent, take leave of their sweethearts, on the pretence of going off to the war; a cynical old pedagogue, who is quite up to snuff as to the situation, stands by and can hardly keep his countenance. Here we have sincere pathos on one side, mock-heroic bathos on the other, with sardonic derision in the middle. This little scene Mozart has set to just three pages of music (full score) which, while duly accentuating every emotion and doing the fullest justice to the humourous side of the situation, is as divinely angelic as anything ever put upon paper; on hearing it you simply feel that

> . . . he on honey-dew hath fed,
> And drunk the milk of Paradise.

"Angelic" is the only word for a good deal in Mozart's music; yet you never feel any lack of a good solid foundation of warm human flesh and blood.

As the due psychical counterpoise to this idealizing bent, Mozart had a practical clear-headedness that almost seeks its fellow in history; and, like most thoroughly clear-headed men, he had a phenomenally retentive and accurate memory. Immediate decision and the consequent retention of a perfectly distinct mental picture of what he had decided upon were perhaps his most prominent mental traits. His peculiar method of composing shows this. When about to compose a movement, he would rule off page after page of score-paper with bars; then he would write down (either completely or sketchily, as the case might be) some sixteen, eighteen, or twenty-four measures of music, then skip a certain number of measures (always carefully counted) and go on from there. His first draft would thus be full of lacunæ; and, in afterwards filling these out, he would seldom have to add or subtract a single measure of this skeleton, nor would the passages already written undergo any alteration. What had been the first draft would become the finished copy; he seldom made another.

The story that he wrote a large part of *Don*

Giovanni on a table in a public beer-garden, between turns at bowling, is probably true, certainly characteristic. The fact is that Mozart hardly ever made what other composers would call a preliminary sketch; he would elaborate a whole composition in his head before putting pen to paper at all, so that his actual writing was little more than copying from memory. And this he could very well do under circumstances that would have been utterly unfavourable to thinking out a composition.*

Mozart wrote, first and last, some twelve Italian and five German operas and operettas.

---

* This habitual method of composing is a far stronger proof of the power of Mozart's musical memory than the oft-told story of his writing the horn, trumpet, and kettle-drum parts of the overture to *Don Giovanni* after sending of the MS. score, containing only the string and wood-wind parts, to the copyist. A tolerable feat of memory this certainly was, especially as the whole overture was written in a single night, and so hurriedly that he had no time to look over the first section of the score before sending it off. But it sinks into insignificance beside Wagner's ruling off the bars for his clean copy of the whole first act of the *Meistersinger*, without once referring to his first copy, and finding that he had allowed just the right amount of space for the notes of every measure in the whole act. Neither was Mozart's memory quite so accurate in the case mentioned; for just before the first performance, there having been no time to rehearse the overture, he had to say to the orchestra: "Gentlemen of the brass and drums, at one point you will find in your parts either four measures too many, or four too few, I can't now remember which; but, if you follow my beat, all will come right!"

The first performed was *Bastien und Bastienne*, a one-act piece, the text of which was adapted by Anton Schacht from Weiskern's translation of a parody on Jean-Jacques's *Devin du village* written by madame Favart—rather a complicated authorship. This little *Singspiel* was given in Vienna in the summer-house of Mozart's friends, the Missmers, in 1768, the composer being then twelve years old.* His last opera, *Die Zauberflöte*,—the libretto by Emanuel Schikaneder, manager of the theatre,—was brought out at the Theatre an der Wieden on September 30, 1791, the year of the composer's death. Thus Mozart's career as an opera-composer began and ended with German works.

This fact has, however, no real significance; he did his greatest work in Italian Opera. There was, upon the whole, a great deal of the Italian in Mozart, as a musician, even more than in Handel. He had the German depth of *Gemüth*, the Teutonic seriousness and artistic conscientiousness; but in all else he was (musically) Italian to the core. His caste of me-

---

* Curiously enough, the principal theme of the overture is, note for note, the same as the opening theme of Beethoven's *Eroica* symphony—only, in G major instead of E-flat major. Was this a mere coincidence, or had Beethoven seen a score of *Bastien und Bastienne?* At all events, the Thunderer had a way of taking his own wherever he found it.

lody is distinctly Italian ; nothing in all Opera is more foreign to what is known as " German singing " than his music—whether to German or Italian words. And what is true of his vocal writing is true of his instrumental compositions.* Notably Italian was his complete and facile mastery in *recitativo secco*, that free form of colloquial recitative that is accompanied by a 'cello and double-bass, with a few improvised chords struck by the cembalist ; no Italian, not even Rossini himself, could beat him in this line. It may have been a keen appreciation of the perfection of this style as a musical medium for familiar dialogue, and of the utter inadaptability of the German language to anything of the sort, that induced him to accept the conventional bastard form of the German *Spieloper*—set musical numbers connected by spoken dialogue—for his German operas. That he made no attempt to develop a corresponding form of German recitative is a fact.

That Mozart came into the world without a manifesto, and quitted it leaving none behind him, that he showed on occasion a singularly

---

* Hans von Bülow was once heard to say : "I had rather hear an average first-rate Italian or French violinist play the first violin part in a Mozart quartet than any but two or three of my respected fellow-countrymen."

easy-going contentedness with even the worst conventions of his day, should not be taken as evidence that he did nothing new ; in principle he may have done little, but in fact he did a good deal. His enormous development of the act-finale, the only item in which the Opera in his hands approached the character of the Wagnerian Music-Drama, was in itself something unprecedented. In general, however, what may be called his musical formula was as unlike Wagner's, or that of the old Florentines, as possible ; it has been found no little fault with of late years, and people have marvelled at his achievement of such stupendous results with so poor a tool.

But his formula was really not quite so poor as all that ; it suited his artistic purpose to a T. And we should not forget that Mozart's task, in other words, the class of libretti he had to deal with, was radically different from Wagner's.

Wagner, notably in his later works, had to deal with the Drama of Continuous Development ; the action goes on continuously from the beginning to the end of an act ; nothing is omitted, there are no lacunæ in its logic ; either it rises by gradual climax to a culminating point at the close of the act, or else this culmination comes earlier, to be followed by a period of subsidence which in turn leads over to the point of departure for a fresh climax. In either case, there is no breach of continuity.

In the texts of Mozart's best operas, on the other hand, we find nothing of the sort. The libretto presents a mere succession of situations the logical connection between any two of which is either but summarily hinted at in the dialogue, or else, left wholly to the spectator's perception. The dramatic development is nowhere continuous, but proceeds by fits and starts, until we come to a short period of continuity near the end of an act. No doubt the several situations in the above-mentioned succession are culled from an ideal continuous climax, and each one comes in in its proper order; but the logical connection is omitted. Whereas, in the Wagnerian Drama, the account given of the action is fully itemized, like that in a business man's day-book, that given in the Mozart libretti is like the one to be found in the second column of a ledger, consisting of a series of partial results, with most of the separate items omitted. Nevertheless, by supplying the logical connection for himself, the spectator can obtain a certain sense of climax, much as the listener to pianoforte-playing can get a sense of sustained melody from what is really nothing more than a series of well-ordered accents, without sustained musical tone. But, for him to obtain this sense of essential climax, the succession must be rapid; and this indispensable rapidity we surely do find in the Mozart libretti, as we do also in Shakspere's plays.

Now, Mozart's musical formula—a succession of set musical numbers (solos, duets, ensemble-pieces, etc.), with intervening stretches of *secco* recitative—corresponds exactly to the dramatic formula of his librettists. Such a formula would be ridiculous if applied to texts like *Tristan und Isolde* or the *Meistersinger*, as much out of place as the Wagnerian formula would be with such libretti as *Figaro* or *Don Giovanni;* but with these latter libretti it works to perfection, the sense for artistic fitness is completely satisfied.

Mozart's greatest opera is unquestionably *Don Giovanni* (the text adapted by the abbate Lorenzo da Ponte from Molière's *Festin de pierre*, first given, under the composer's personal direction, at Prag on October 29, 1787). *Die Zauberflöte* is pulled down from this high plane by its weak text—of which no one but a Free Mason can make head or tail—while *Le nozze di Figaro* (the libretto also by da Ponte, after Beaumarchais, brought out at the Vienna Burgtheater on May 1, 1786) lapses nearly as far by reason of a certain failure on the composer's part to enter fully and sympathetically into the "tone" of his subject. Mozart was

great, but not quite universal; keen as was his
sense of humour, Beaumarchais's spirit of ma-
licious raillery was not in his nature, he could
not twist his features into that sardonic, *scha-
denfrohe* smile.*

Curiously enough, *Don Giovanni*, though long
one of the most popular,† is nowadays one of
the least correctly appreciated of operas. Few
operas are habitually given so radically and ruin-
ously wrong. Both in Europe and this country
Don Giovanni is usually given in vast court or me-
tropolitan opera-houses, with orchestras double
or treble the size intended by Mozart (a most
necessary evil, this last, for Mozart's orchestra
would be utterly lost in a large theatre). ‡ To
counteract these two false conditions, the music
is sung, for the most part, with all the stress of
voice, all the flamboyant vociferation that be-

---

* In this respect, and this respect alone, Rossini's *Barbiere* is
far better in tune with the Beaumarchais original than Mozart's
Figaro.

† " Let me tell you that the ' Don Giovanni ' had the greatest suc-
cess of any opera which has been brought forward, in my time, in
America."—MAX MARETZEK, *Crotchets and Quavers*, page 102.
New York, 1855.

‡ At Covent Garden in London, Sir Michael Costa used to add
trombones, tuba, and bass-drum and cymbals in the stretto of the
first finale ; and doubling the solo voices with a chorus in some
portions of this same finale is customary everywhere, save at one
theatre in Germany.

long to " grand " Opera. That certain scenes
may be set effectively, the original two acts
have been cut up into three and four, and long-
ish waits come between some scenes, thus de-
stroying that rapidity of succession which is
indispensable to the sense of climax. Indeed,
the vast opera-houses, big orchestras, the general style of singing, and the tragic grandeur
of the closing statue-scene, have all united to
give many, perhaps most, opera-goers the impression that *Don Giovanni* is a grand opera.

This impression is radically wrong; up to
the last scene, *Don Giovanni* is an *opera buffa*—
it is styled " *dramma giocoso* " on the title-page.
It is comedy of the most intimately subtle sort,
requiring a very small house and orchestra, that
no deft play of feature, no nimbly significant
gesture, no delicately expressive shading of the
voice may be lost upon the audience. Its gist,
as Verlaine would say, lies in the nuance, not in
the colour; it is a work of the finest subtlety,
not of hammer-and-tongs. Then, the original
cut of acts and scenes must be scrupulously
preserved, and one scene follow hard upon the
heels of another; the iron must never be allowed
to cool off, the audience, never be given a moment's breathing-time. Only at the little Resi-
denztheater in Munich is *Don Giovanni* so given
nowadays, with all the librettist's and com-

poser's intentions scrupulously carried out—
only, what must the singing be ?

In *Don Giovanni* Mozart's power of character-
drawing shows itself in all its glory. If, in
Figaro, he has idealized some of the characters
out of all semblance to their original selves, in
Don Giovanni this idealizing process has been
carried on on lines exactly parallel with the
original bent of the several *dramatis personæ*,
and serves but more highly to potentize their
individuality. Without losing a whit of their
identity, without being one jot less sharply individualized, they rise to the stature of universal and eternal types.

To take but one example from out of several,
think what it means for a composer to reflect
the whole of so profoundly and eternally significant a character as Don Juan—to the very
heart of his heart, and to the marrow of his
bones—in that elusive mirror we call Music !
And this, too, in the jaunty, lightly-tripping
dialect of *opera buffa !* This miracle Mozart
works through nearly two long acts ; then, with
sudden flight, he soars up to the loftiest sublime
of awful grandeur when, wrong and retribution
having met face to face to try conclusions with
each other, his hero, long the incarnation of
tragedy to fellow-mortals, has at last become
tragic to himself.

In this second finale Mozart shows whither his genius could lead him on an emergency; here he suddenly discards his familiar methods and instinctively takes—to be sure, in his own way and style—to the Wagner method. One foot thrust over the wall of the Future into the midst of Beethoven's *Eroica*, is it? Aye, and more than that, into the midst of the Wagnerian Music-Drama.

So far did Mozart bring it in Opera; with a mighty outstretch of his arms, he clasped hands with Handel and Wagner. But, save for the richness of the legacy he left the world, he really affected the history of Opera not a whit. After his death, the opera-writing world went its own way, as if he had not been. After 1787, the year of *Don Giovanni*, nothing so essentially "modern" in conception and style as the statue-scene made its appearance on the lyric stage until 1865, the year of Wagner's *Tristan und Isolde*.

V

The Italians

THE typical opera-composer in Italy during the last quarter of the eighteenth century was Domenico Cimarosa—born at Aversa, near Naples, on December 17, 1749, died in Venice on April 5, 1801. Every inch a musical dramatist born and bred, a consummate master of musical form, Cimarosa may be said to have summed up in himself Italian *opera seria* and *opera buffa* from the fading out of the last remnants of the Scarlatti school up to the advent of Rossini.

The general aspect of Cimarosa's work is very like that of Mozart's; his style is simpler, his musical developments are less extended, his forms less varied, his use of the orchestra is less poetic and picturesque; but the general physiognomy of his operas is much the same. His fame was universal; his *Matrimonio segreto* (given first in Vienna in 1792, a year after Mozart's death) was, in the opinion of the time, the first *opera buffa* to dispute the thitherto unquestioned supremacy in that field of Pergolesi's *Serva padrona*. For over a generation, *Il matrimonio segreto* was regarded as incarnating the highest ideal of *opera buffa*. Cimarosa was great, too, in *opera seria ;* his *Gli Orazj e Curiazj* (Venice, 1794) can stand as one of the strongest heroic operas of its day.

But, upon the whole, Cimarosa is chiefly interesting now as a type of his epoch; he had not, like Mozart, the genius that survives, his operas could not long outlive the changes of fashion. Rossini fairly blew his light out.

In passing from Cimarosa to the next generation of composers in Italy, we are struck with what seems very like a disruption of continuity in the evolution of Italian Opera ; with Rossini's arrival upon the stage its general aspect, its whole physiognomy, seem to undergo a sudden transformation. The fact is that, even before Rossini, the great Italian musical decadence of the first half of the nineteenth century, destined soon to acquire a terrific momentum, was already setting in. Instrumental composition had for some time been entirely neglected in Italy, save in the one matter of the opera overture, or *sinfonia ;* * the old glory of Italian

---

* So exclusively had this term become associated with the opera overture in Italy that, when the present *Società del Quartetto* began its symphony concerts in Florence, the only intelligible way it

Church Music was still upheld by the chevalier Sarti (1729–1802) alone; after him it went
pretty well to the dogs.* The only form cultivated with any enthusiasm was the Opera.
The Italian operatic conquest of the then musical world was complete; Italian Opera, sung
by Italian singers, was an established fact in
France, Germany, and England, and held its
own well in competition with the home-made
article. Italy had become authorized operatic
purveyor to the world, especially to the aristocratic, fashion-setting part thereof. But, with
all this enormous production and exportation
of operas, Italy had stopped importing anything whatsoever of the musical sort; even
musical ideas were stopped at the frontier.
Italy held herself absolutely aloof from the
great new musical development then going forward with giant strides in Germany, shut herself up within her own boundaries, and depended wholly upon her own resources. The
result was a sort of musical in-breeding that
made a disastrous drain upon the artistic sta-
mina of the nation, utterly uncompensated for

could find to describe a Haydn symphony on its programs was :
"*sinfonia classica in quattro pezzi.*"

* Fétis called Sarti "the last of the great Italian contrapuntists;" to which his bosom friend, and Sarti's pupil, Cherubini
may be fancied as muttering "last *but one !*"

by the introduction of any fresh foreign strain. The country was sapping its musical strength with a vengeance!

Everything suffered; Italian musical instruction deteriorated, neither was it much heeded; for the younger generation began running away from conservatories before its technical education was half completed, so that the whole musical production of the country soon began to labour under the most terrible handicap that can be set upon any kind of creative art, a defective and inadequate technique. It did not take a generation for the Italians to fall, as musical craftsmen, immeasurably behind the Germans, whom they had once taught. The whole musical standard was lowered, and the land which had once produced such unsurpassed experts in technics as Palestrina, Giovanni Gabrieli, and the Naninis, plunged down into the ignominy of looking upon poor Saverio Mercadante as (heaven save the mark!) a "*gran' contrappuntista.*" Let no one rant about the glory of pure genius and Music's speaking to the heart; the truth that can not be got round is that a general deterioration in technical ability, in the ability to do, in any nation is a sure diagnostic symptom of artistic decay.

One finds in the generation of Italian composers that came after Cimarosa a marked technical falling off, evinced in a general impoverishment and stunting of the musical forms employed. Especially noteworthy is the monotonous paucity of these forms. The only thorough technical mastery shown is an admirable skill in treating the human voice, and in handling the orchestra so as to make the voice effective. Save for this, the best that can be said of these composers, technically speaking, is that, with the keen practical instinct of genius, they adapted themselves wonderfully well to the situation, and attempted no tasks beyond their powers. Genius surely was not lacking! But with this generation came about the great split between Italian and German Music—operatic and otherwise; up to and including Cimarosa, the difference between the two schools had been one of national temperament mainly; now it grew into a wider and wider divergence of artistic aim and style. Before long, German Music got to be utterly unintelligible to the average Italian, who, whether it was a drinking-song, a symphony, or an opera finale, shrugged his shoulders and lumped it all indiscriminately together as " *musica di chiesa* (church-music)."

The period we now come to was illustrated by several composers of high genius, of whom let the following five be mentioned:—

Gioacchino Rossini, born at Pesaro in the Romagna on February 29, 1792.

Saverio Mercadante, born at Altamura, near Bari, on December 17, 1795.

Giovanni Pacini, born at Catania in Sicily on February 19, 1796.

Gaëtano Donizetti, born at Bergamo on November 29, 1797.

Vincenzo Bellini, born at Catania on November 13, ~~1802~~. 1801

Rossini was the head and front of the whole movement. Pacini, Donizetti, and Bellini were, in one sense, followers of his, in another, reactionaries against his dominant tendency.* This last fact has too often been overlooked.

What Rossini chiefly did was to perpetuate far into the nineteenth century—and with immense genius, too—every deplorable vice the Opera had contracted in its Venetian and Neapolitan periods. True, he dressed up these vices, with inexhaustible originality, in a new garb, but he did not cure them of their deformity. The *opera buffa* was a thing too much after his own heart for him not to enter naturally and sympathetically into its spirit; but in *opera*

---

* Mercadante deserves mention only *honoris causa*, as ultimately the dean of the school; he outlived the others, dying at the age of seventy-five in 1870.

seria he let all dramatic and scenic considerations go hang with a reckless insouciance that seeks its fellow, and played into the virtuoso singer's hand with a frankness that left nothing to be desired.

A man of the most fertile melodic inventiveness, of incomparable brilliancy, gifted with a facility that can fairly be called damnable, Rossini enthroned graceful Frivolity in the centre of the lyric stage, to rule autocratically over singers and orchestra. Cavalli was nothing to him! His serious Italian operas have, to be sure, the advantage of greater superficial variety over those of the older Scarlatti-Handel school; instead of an unbroken string of recitatives and arias, they present a motley succession of airs, duets, concerted pieces, and finales. But in intrinsic dramatic and scenic quality they hardly excel those of the Neapolitan school of the first half of the eighteenth century, while their musical style is far less distinguished. *Semiramide* (Venice, 1823) is little better than a two-act concert in costume; and staid choral societies in this country found no difficulty, in the 'forties and 'fifties, in making *Mosè in Egitto* (Naples, 1818) go down as an oratorio. No doubt the lack of dramatic quality in the Rossini *opera seria* is not quite so total as some people nowadays would make it

ROSSINI.

out to be; much depends upon the style of singing, and the old " grand " style of *coloratura*-singing—not over-fast, with full voice and dramatic stress of accent—virtually went out a good many years ago.* It is a fact that Semiramide used to rank in its day as a strong dramatic soprano part.

Rossini simply ran *coloratura, fioritura*, the trill, roulade, and every form of vocal ornamentation into the ground; even his recitatives are full of such things. He had, upon the whole, greater fondness for bright and sprightly rhythms than for sustained, expressive *cantilena*; true, he gave to the world some exquisite masterpieces of broadly-phrased melody,—the once-famous swan-song, " *Assisa al piè d'un salice*," of Desdemona in *Otello* (Naples, 1816) among them,—but he preferred the nimbler tempi, and often reduced the *cavatina* of an aria to the dimensions of a mere introduction to the closing rondo.

It was, however, in *opera buffa* that Rossini was most royally at home and did his greatest

---

* Some of the present older generation can still remember sporadic instances of it : Euphrosyne Parepa, Therese Tietjens, Gabrielle Krauss; its last living exponent is Lilli Lehmann. The break-neck vocal agility of the strings-of-pearls, canary-bird style of warbling came in with Maria Piccolomini and Angiolina Bosio in the 'fifties, and has thriven to the detriment of the other since.

work. Of the delicate Mozartian subtlety he had little, he laid on the colours thicker. But the true comic verve he had to perfection; a deal of what the French call "*malice*," too; Offenbach himself is not cuter. The sparkle of his melodies, the overbrimming humour of his recitatives, the brilliancy of his orchestra, with the champagne-fizzing of its violin triplets and the irresistible dash of its *crescendo*,* all place him in the very foremost rank of *buffo* composers. After all and with all his faults, he was the greatest musical genius Italy had produced since Alessandro Scarlatti.

It seems strange now that his *Barbiere di Siviglia*, surely the most sparkling *opera buffa* ever written, if not the greatest, was damned outright by the public when it was brought out at the Argentina in Rome in 1816; but this has ever been the way with entirely great works. Perhaps, of Rossini's whole bag and baggage, this *Barbiere* is the one opera that is destined to live into this century; in it he shows himself at his very best. In Don Basilio's "*La calunnia è un venticello*" he rises to a pitch of in-

---

* The famous "Rossini" *crescendo*—two measures in the tonic, repeated in the dominant, the whole gone over three times with ever-increasing force—was not really his invention. The earliest instance of it known to the present author is in Beethoven's overture to *Leonore* (so-called) No. 1, written in 1807.

trinsic dramatic force that is hardly outdone by anything in *Guillaume Tell*.* The *Barbiere* may fairly be called immortal; its brilliance has certainly suffered no tarnish yet. Rossini died in Paris on November 13, 1868; for brilliancy, dash, and a certain easy-going, ingenuous artistic rascality (not a deeply premeditated rascality, like Meyerbeer's), the world will probably never look upon his like again!†

No composer goes to such extremes in any one direction as Rossini did, without a reaction setting in sooner or later. In his case, the reaction came soon enough, even before his career was over. A form of art like the Opera has a hard time of it ridding itself of the influence of tradition; the Italian Opera, in especial, had traditions enough of its own. Two of the oldest of these, indeed they dated back to the very inception of the form, were expressive melody and vocal ornamentation. ‡ It was, accord-

---

* As is usual with such gems, the authenticity of the " *Calunnia* " has been called in question; the only answer to which doubt is the counter-question: Who else under the sun *could* have written it?

† All consideration of *Guillaume Tell*, generally accepted as Rossini's greatest work, must come in the chapter devoted to the French School.

‡ If what we now call melody was considerably lacking in the first Florentine operas, it was simply because melody, in our sense of the word, had not then been developed; but emotionally ex-

ingly, no wonder that Rossini's younger contemporaries,—who, after all, based their style
mainly upon his,—noting his florid excesses,
should have felt

> Of two such lessons, why forget
> The nobler and the manlier one?

The first to react against the over-floridness
of Rossini's style was Pacini. He preached and
practised a return to the "grand old Italian
tradition" of expressive *cantilena*. A man of
high repute in his day, he is totally forgotten
now; the stronger dramatic genius of Donizetti and Bellini gradually threw him into the
shade, and his works soon grew old-fashioned.
Of his seventy-five operas, *Saffo* (Naples, 1840)
held the stage longest. It was more by his artistic attitude than by his genius that he won a
lasting place in history.

After Rossini, the strongest men of the period were unquestionably Donizetti and Bellini.
Their contemporary fame was by no means
equal to his—Rossini's world-conquest was im-

---

pressive vocal writing was the back-bone of the form from the
first, and the then composers made it as melodious as they knew
how—just as the early Florentine painters copied Nature as
closely as they knew how. As for vocal ornamentation, only remember the Archilei's "*gruppi e lunghi giri*," mentioned by Peri
in his *Euridice* preface.

mediate and overwhelming; the slow rise of Richard Wagner in our time, was as nothing, compared to his " *Veni, vidi, vici !* "—but they still held their own well, side by side with him, and eventually showed a greater power of survival. Their genius was more essentially dramatic than his. Perhaps it were wrong to say that they had more dramatic power than he could show, at a pinch; but the dramatic instinct, the dramatic mood, was more habitual with them. They were men of constitutionally warmer feeling than he.

One can hardly find another pair of composers whose artistic nature and work exhibit such curious inconsistencies. In this respect, they are far more characteristic types of the Italian Opera of their period than Rossini himself. From whatever point of view they may be considered, it must be owned in the end that their genius was distinctly emotional and dramatic; they had the reddest of blood in their veins, and a very poignant faculty of expression. Yet the musical forms in which they worked were, for the most part, quite as undramatic and unscenic as Rossini's. Their succeeding in being dramatic in spite of it all, is perhaps the best proof of the quality of their genius. Then, take their style. In one sense, it was simplicity and naturalness itself, even verging, in Bellini's

case, dangerously on *niaiserie*.* But, in another
sense, it was as sophisticated, as full of what the
French call *raffinement*, as any known to history;
especially so in the matter of expression, in
which it often pinched itself to absolute preciosity. With them, the frankest outpouring of
genuinely warm emotion went hand in hand
with a calculated appeal to a highly cultured
taste. But their passion was none the less real
for all this super-refined preciosity of expression; all the rose-water they poured upon it
could not quench its flame.

Of the two, Donizetti had the larger scope,
the more virile nature. He was also the more
careless and unequal. But, at his best, he had
no mean power. Few things on the lyric stage
are more admirably brilliant in the way of dramatic characterization than the prologue of his
Lucrezia Borgia (Milan, 1834); the music gives
you the very quintessence of the Venetian life of
the period—its luxurious insouciance, its atmosphere of intrigue, its undercurrent of hot passion; it is Paolo Veronese in Music! Light
music enough, if you will, but full of matter.
Lucrezia is probably his best opera, though
Lucia di Lammermoor (Naples, 1835) has had

---

* It was in reference to Bellini that the late Julius Eichberg
once said: "Clarity is a precious thing; but there is no artistic need of music's being *clearer* than crystal!"

more recognition outside of Italy; but in *Lucrezia* he strikes and sustains a more original note, there is more brilliancy and snap, a fiercer dramatic blaze. For one thing, as a piece of musical character-drawing,—in the Mozart and Wagner sense, — Maffeo Orsini (in *Lucrezia*) overtops anything else of the sort done in the whole period; the elegant, devil-may-care young rake lives and breathes before you!

Donizetti also did admirable work in *opera buffa;* his *Don Pasquale* (Paris, 1843), though by no means quite in the Rossini vein, can rank with any of Rossini's, save the *Barbiere* alone.

But there was not a spark of fun in Bellini; he was great only in *opera seria*. Despite a certain besetting effeminacy of sentiment, too, too naïve at times, he rises now and then to an impressive grandeur of which one finds little in Donizetti. *Norma* (Milan, 1831) has generally been accounted his masterpiece,* and it is perhaps the opera in which he most rose out of his ordinary self. But *La sonnambula* is more characteristic, in a more congenial vein; it is a chef-d'œuvre of sensibility. In this charming opera (brought out in Milan in the same year as *Norma*) Bellini best shows his peculiar melo-

---

* Schopenhauer has brought forward the libretto of *Norma* (by Felice Romani) as an unsurpassed example of the dramatic treatment of a tragic subject.

dic power ; few melodies give a stronger pluck to the heartstrings—yet wholly without passionateness; expressing merely the vibrant *joie de vivre* of innocent, love-struck sweet sixteen—than Amina's " *Come per me sereno oggi rinacque il dì !* " Here, as also in the foregoing recitative, " *Care compagne,*" we have something of Gluck's tear-provoking power of expressing perfect happiness.

Of course, in Donizetti's and Bellini's day, no composers in their senses would have bitten their own noses off by reacting too radically against Rossini's florid style ; these two Italians were no Richard Wagners, and knew enough not to set the whole race of singers against them by a too ascetic return to merely expressive *cantilena*. They wrote vocal flourishes galore; but theirs were, for the most part, the natural efflorescence of an originally simple melody, which, in their hands, blossomed out into flowery bedizenment, like the apple-branches in spring; the *fioritura* is purely ornamental, not the main business in hand, as it was too often with Rossini.

Upon the whole, though, it was rather a debilitating business, this Opera of sweet sentiment, beautiful melody, and ear-tickling; a matter of exquisite taste rather than of sturdy artistic vitality. For one thing, it eventually became the theme of probably the worst musical literature (written by amateurs) the world has ever had to blush for.

Into the midst of all this rose-water preciosity suddenly sprang Giuseppe Verdi!

No man ever came into the world at a fitter moment; everything was just ready for him. Even the most delicate palates had begun to cloy with the Donizetti-Bellini syrup, and to yearn for a tarter fillip; and Verdi, of all men in the world, was the one to give it them. A born son of the people,—his parents were innkeepers in the smallest of ways at the little hamlet of Roncole, near Busseto in Parma,— the hottest-blooded man of passion the Art of Music had known since Beethoven, Verdi came into Italian Opera as a veritable *sansculotte*. His was a voice from the nether stratum, frank, fierce, lurid, unheard before on the lyric stage; he brought into over-sophisticated Opera the popular song (or something very like it), and turned its siren warblings to passionate utterance,—his detractors said, to screaming. His volcanic heat fairly singed the boards; people began to wake up, and say: Here verily is a man!

Verdi was no better technician than the others, no more inclined to be squeamish about old conventions. He took the Opera quite as he found it; only, he breathed into it a new spirit. The most hopelessly reticent man in private life, the despair of prying reporters, in his art Verdi unbuttoned freely, was outspokenness itself; what he said was unmistakable, no composer in the whole list ever had less reserve. He was absolutely fearless in going to all lengths, had no respect at all for any sort of Mrs. Grundy, and, at first, little disposition to be self-critical; his genius, always of a rather sombre cast, carried him by fits and starts from majestic dignity or courtly elegance to the depths of triviality and vulgarity; to one thing alone was he ever constant: to his own genuineness. In time he became at once the most popular and the most decried operacomposer alive; the musical plebs swore by him, while to musicians (especially outside of Italy) his name was a by-word for everything artistically reprehensible. To sum him up in a sentence, he was the diametrical antithesis of Felix Mendelssohn.

Apart from the force of his genius, the most noteworthy thing about Verdi has been his incomparable and never-flagging power of artistic growth. He was born on October 9, 1813, and is still living. This length of life has given him the opportunity, which surely few would have exploited as well as he, to have four di-

VERDI.

stinct periods, or manners—most great composers stop at their third! In his earlier operas—*Nabucco* (Milan, 1842), *I Lombardi alla prima crociata* (ib., 1843), *Ernani* (Venice, 1844), *I due Foscari* (Rome, 1844), up to *Luisa Miller* (Naples, 1849)—he shows, with all his melodic power, a certain formal stiffness; as good an example of this as another is Zaccaria's aria with chorus, "*D'Egitto là sui lidi*," in *Nabucco*, a grandly broad melody, not without impressive majesty, but still breathing something of well-starched, "official" formalism; it is a little academic. With *Rigoletto* (Venice, 1851) his style grows more elastic, his melody freer and more original, his passion and dramatic fire burn at their hottest. In this second period come his most popular, as well as, in one sense, his most characteristic operas: *Il trovatore* (Rome, 1853), *La traviata* (Venice, 1853), *Un ballo in maschera* (Rome, 1859), and a few others of less note. Strangely enough, this second manner of Verdi's has none of those transitional characteristics that mark the second period of most composers; his style is individual and fully formed, his technique, if not conspicuous by any high standard, is yet his own and entirely adequate to its task. Noteworthy is a certain relaxing of the curb of strict form, perhaps due in some measure to the Meyerbeer influence, which had by that time well made the round of Europe ; in the last scene in the *Trovatore* (surely one of the greatest he ever wrote) we already find the musical form conditioned by hardly anything save a dramatic conception of the text ; in this respect, the scene was twenty years in advance of all else done in Italy at the time.

The apparent finality of Verdi's second manner was, however, deceptive ; the man had by no means got to the end of his tether yet! His third was really his transition period—*La forza del destino* (St. Petersburg, 1862), *Don Carlos* (Paris, 1867), *Aïda* (Cairo, 1871). Here we find distinctly French influence at work, also a touch of the "new romantic" Liszt-Berlioz-Wagner eleutheromania. *Aïda* may well be compared, as a transitional work, with Wagner's *Lohengrin ;* side by side with much that is conventional, the final (fourth) manner is more than foreshadowed in it. In this period Verdi's style becomes vastly more complex; you find him taking unwonted pains with himself, with his orchestra, with larger and more complex musical developments, with the finer subtleties of dramatic expression and local colour. In a word, though still thoroughly an Italian, Verdi evinces a determination not to lag behind with the rest of his countrymen, but to show himself as well abreast of the age.

With *Aïda* we must now leave Verdi for a while; his fourth manner belongs to the present, probably still more to the future. He has been considered here as a man of the Donizetti-Bellini epoch, and as the bridge that led over therefrom to the Italian Opera of to-day.

One thing is, however, important to establish: no matter how intrinsically unscenic were the forms of Italian Opera from Rossini to the "younger" Verdi, the music was distinctly written to be sung with the intensest dramatic stress; herein it differs most fundamentally from that of the old Scarlatti-Handel Opera. Then, a certain amount of dramatic action is not only possible but, so to speak, inevitable in Donizetti's, Bellini's, and Verdi's operas; with a Handel aria it is simply inconceivable. So much scenic quality the music undeniably had. With all its conventional formality, it was really dramatic in its essence. Some very striking examples may be adduced: the quartet, "*Bella figlia*," in *Rigoletto*, where three, aye, four different emotions are expressed simultaneously, and with perfect truth to nature—a feat unparalleled in the annals of Opera! Take, again, the final terzet, "*Ferma, crudele*," in *Ernani*, where the music, though of perfectly regular construction, never for a moment relaxing the strictness of its dance-rhythm, lends itself to every subtle change of expression in the text, and gradually swells to a lava-stream of dramatic impetuosity. Upon the whole, it is quite significant of the fitness of this music for the stage that it loses more than half its zest, and well-nigh collapses, in the concert-room. How and why it fits the stage is not so easy to show, but it certainly does fit it wondrous well in its way.*

* Some points omitted in this chapter—to economize space—are brought up in Chapter VIII. *Vide* foot-note on page 158, concerning the act-finale, and also page 167.

VI

The French School

IF any nation has done its full share toward proving the truth of the saying that, in Opera, the comic is everywhere the more distinctively national form, France has. French *opéra-comique* has been illustrated almost exclusively by native composers, around the heads of many of whom Fame has drawn the aureola of immortality—no matter how perishable Time may have proved their works to be. But, in the list of composers who, for hard upon two centuries, supplied the Académie de Musique —the chosen home of Grand Opera in France —with works, the greatest and most world-famous names are, with one or two exceptions, not French. Rameau may fairly be rated as a first-class man; but the two Bertons (old Pierre-Montan and his son, Henri-Montan), Lesueur, Méhul, Kreutzer, Persuis, Catel, Halévy, and others of less note can not stand in history on a level with Lully, Gluck, Cherubini, Spontini, Rossini, and Meyerbeer. Even

Auber, whose *Muette de Portici* might be taken
as a fairish claim to fellowship with these great
foreigners, did his best and most characteristic
work for the Opéra-Comique, as did also several of his above-mentioned compatriots.

But, such has been the inflexibility of French
taste, of French ideas, so irresistible the force
of French influence, when exerted near-to and
at home, that, with and in spite of all the foreign genius that has been welcomed, first and
last, to the Académie de Musique, the school of
Grand Opera is indefeasibly French. What
may be called the French idea has ruled
throughout. Nevertheless, the high-sweeping
scythe of cursory History will cut off, for the
most part, un-French heads!

Gluck's first successor in Paris was his pupil,
Antonio Salieri, born at Legnano in Venetia on
August 19, 1750, died in Vienna on May 7,
1835. What may be called a first-rate second-
class man, Salieri founded himself entirely upon
Gluck; his *Les Danaïdes* (1784), *Les Horaces*
(1786), *Tarare* (1787), and a few other operas
served to keep the Gluck tradition fresh for
a while. Cherubini, who, unlike most of the
great foreigners, did better work for the Opéra-
Comique than for the Académie de Musique,
may still be mentioned here as filling up the
gap between Salieri and Spontini with his

Démophon (1788), *Anacréon* (1807), and a few intervening operas. Cherubini, however, made something of a temporary break in the Gluck tradition, for he held more by Mozart than by the Viennese reformer.

The thread of the tradition is, however, knotted again by Spontini. Gasparo Spontini (afterwards conte di Sant' Andrea) was born at Majolati in the Marches of Ancona on November 14, 1774, and died there on January 24, 1851. After writing a number of Italian operas of the conventional sort in his native country, he came to Paris in 1803; here he submitted himself willingly to French influence, and his style soon underwent a noteworthy change; it was in Paris that his great, indeed his only considerable, period began. He accepted the Gluck formula *in toto;* temperamentally, too, there was no little resemblance between him and the Vienna master: he had a similar poignancy of feeling, a similar noble reserve in expression, the same at-homeness in the classic atmosphere. His music, however, strongly reflects native Italian influence; in some of his melodies, still more in some of his orchestral passage-work, he even foreshadows Rossini. Upon the whole, he can stand as a very Italian Gluck. He was immeasurably the strongest figure in French Grand Opera

between Gluck and the romantic movement of
1830; his *Vestale* (1807), *Fernand Cortez* (1809),
and *Olympie* (1819) lived well into the second
half of the century both in France and in Germany. He was the last of the great "classi-
cists" of the lyric stage; a man of no mean
grandeur, sombre sublimity, and dramatic
force, one who could be at white heat with
seemingly unmoved countenance. With an
ounce more of genius, of the genius that survives, his works might even now be as viable
as Gluck's own; but, like his older fellow-
countryman, Cimarosa, he fell just short of
this mark, and the romantic movement of 1830
was the beginning of his end.

A form which has stood for over a century
and a quarter with its chief traditions unbroken
—for the Gluck Reform was an enlarging and
consolidating, rather than a breaking, of the
Lully-Rameau traditions — may fairly be regarded as settled. The form of French Grand
Opera, as we find it firmly established in Spontini's time, was, in the main, this: a five-act
libretto, set in musical numbers (airs, duets,
concerted pieces, finales) with the connecting
dialogue in stately accompanied recitative (not
the more glib *recitativo secco* of the Italians),
and with grand ballet-divertissements in the
second and fourth acts. This was the standard

norm, and departures from it were few and insignificant; at the Académie de Musique it was as the law of the Medes and Persians.*

If the Grand Opera—called *tragédie-lyrique* when the libretto conformed to the rules of the classic French *tragédie*—was, in the end, but a quasi-academic adaptation of the Italian *opera seria* to French taste, the *opéra-comique* may be called the natural growth, in French soil, of a slip cut from the Italian *opera buffa*. The Grand Opera exemplified French taste; the *opéra-comique* was a perfectly natural and frank expression of French feeling and instinct. It even came only in part from the Italian *opera buffa;* its other parent was the native French *vaudeville*. Its distinctive feature was the spoken dialogue connecting the set musical numbers; and this owed its origin partly to the *vaudeville*, partly also to the impossibility at the time of finding a viable French equivalent for the Italian *recitativo secco*. In French stage terminology, any opera with spoken dialogue

---

* Such a tradition dies hard, and may, moreover, acquire a considerable social importance. The fiasco of *Tannhäuser* at the Académie de Musique in 1861 was chiefly owing to the rage of the more influential class of patrons at the ballet's coming in the first, instead of in the second act—thus interfering with their precious dinners !

is an *opéra-comique*, no matter what the character of its subject.

Two different sorts, or styles, of *opéra-comique* are to be distinguished: the older and the newer. The one was but a higher development of the *vaudeville*, the other tended more in the direction of Grand Opera. Up to within, roughly speaking, twenty years of the end of the eighteenth century, the works of Philidor (1726–1795), Monsigny (1729–1817), Grétry (1741–1813), Dalayrac (1753–1809), and others of their school were, in general, characterized by exceeding musical simplicity; it was often only by the greater proportion of music in them that they were distinguishable from *vaudevilles;* they were strongly imbued with the French *chanson* spirit. With Méhul (1763–1817), Gluck's pupil and ardent follower, larger musical developments came in; some of the musical numbers, notably the act-finales, might have shown their faces without discredit in Grand Opera.* This tendency was carried farther by Boieldieu (1775–1834)—whose *Dame blanche* (1825) is probably the only *opéra-comique* of the first quarter of the nineteenth century practi-

---

* It is significant that, some years ago, there was talk in Paris of the Académie de Musique making an exchange with the Opéra-Comique, the former to exchange Auber's *Le philtre* (which was its property) for Méhul's *Joseph* (owned by the Opéra-Comique).

cally known to most readers of this book—and reached its culmination (that is, without over-stepping the bounds of the style) with Auber (1784–1871) and Hérold (1791–1833). There are many things in works like Auber's *Fra Diavolo* (1830), *Les diamants de la couronne* (1841), or *Haydée* (1847), or Hérold's *Zampa* (1831) or *Le pré aux clercs* (1832) that would not be out of place at the Académie de Musique.

After 1791 these two styles of *opéra-comique* were respectively represented by two rival theatres: the Théâtre Favart (now the Théâtre de l'Opéra-Comique) cultivating the older, classical style, the Théâtre-Feydeau, the newer, more elaborate one. To be sure, no very sharp line of demarcation can be drawn between the two styles; you can find hints at the newer even as far back as Grétry, and many operas savour of both. Probably the composer most on the fence between them was Luigi Cherubini (1760–1842), whose *Médée* (1797), though given at the Feydeau, is virtually a grand opera, and whose *Les deux journées*—known here as *The Water Carrier*, and admittedly his masterpiece—carries the old style to almost *vaudeville* simplicity in all the music but the act-finales, and in these presents developments of an extent and complexity quite worthy of the most elaborate form of Grand Opera. Indeed it is probably owing, as Hanslick shrewdly surmised, to Cherubini's pushing both principles to such extremes, thus showing the contrast between them as so glaring, that a work of the exquisite genius of *Les deux journées* has failed to hold the boards all over the musical world to this day. It fell down between two stools!

The change destined to be worked in French Grand Opera by the romantic ideas, generally known as of 1830, began in 1828, when Auber's *La muette de Portici* (better known here as *Masaniello*) was brought out at the Académie de Musique on February 29. This in every sense epoch-making work came like a thunder-clap out of the blue. Auber, who had hitherto written only for the Opéra-Comique, now brought all the brisk, nimble dash of his style to bear upon a tragic subject, and a subject, too, taken straight from the heart of the people —as Wagner, somewhat too satirically, said: "a revolution of fishermen and costermongers"—with no halo of classic grandeur about it, but white hot with the breath of the proletariat. And his treatment fitted the subject to a T; he outdid himself, showing unwonted dramatic fire, picturesqueness in his orchestra, and a skilful handling of choral masses (that is, dramatically) worthy of the ablest Italians

of the seventeenth century. The old regular
forms of air, duet, etc., are still there; but managed with such deftness, so full of dramatic appositeness, that they are hardly noticed as such.
Eminently the most *brilliant* work the stage of
the Académie de Musique had ever known.

Hard upon the heels of *La muette* followed,
on August 3, 1829, Rossini's *Guillaume Tell*, an
opera which may aptly be described as the effort of the composer's life. Effort is the word!
Here, too, was a romantic subject, taken from
the life of the people, or at least, from popular
(not antique) Legend, the dramatic form bor-
rowed from Schiller's *Wilhelm Tell*. For his
musical treatment of this theme Rossini surely
needed no more brilliancy than he had by nature; but, after thrilling the public of the Académie de Musique with revamped versions of
two of his harum-scarum Italian operas,—*Le
siège de Corinthe* (1826) and *Moïse en Egypte*
(1827),*—he now took himself more seriously,
came over to the French school as far as lay
within his Italian nature, took infinite pains
with all he had hitherto been careless about,
and produced a work worthy of a great genius.
Like Auber before him, he outdid himself, if
not quite in the same way.

---

* Respectively, remodelled versions of *Maometto II* (Naples,
1820) and *Mosè in Egitto* (ib., 1818).

The effort seems to have been somewhat too much for him. At least, how else explain the singular course he pursued after it, a course absolutely without parallel in history? When he wrote *Guillaume Tell*, Rossini was thirty-seven, a strong man in perfect health and spirits; he lived thirty-nine years longer, to the age of seventy-six, and *Tell* was his last opera, almost his last composition of any sort! His thus throwing up an incomparably brilliant career, at a time when he hardly can be said to have attained to the full development of his powers, can not possibly have been owing to Louis-Philippe's government refusing to ratify a contract he had made with Charles X; no man of his flibbertigibbet humour could have stuck to his huff so long as all that! The only plausible explanation is that, after *Tell*, his pride would not allow him to return to his earlier Italian manner,—he had a keen eye for signs of the times, and these were not consoling,—while the prospect of the hard work needed to produce more *Tells* was more than his laziness could stomach. He is the only great composer on record who ever abdicated in the prime of life; he preferred not writing at all to not writing easily.

Unfortunately for both *La muette* and *Guillaume Tell*, they were, with all their force of

genius, all their come-outer boldness, merely
transitional works; moreover, the particular
march of progress they had set in motion so
soon acquired speed and momentum that they
found it doubly hard to hold their own against
it. It is no mean testimony to their intrinsic
strength that they held out as long as they did;
they have not quite lapsed from the repertory
yet. But they were quick in growing old-
fashioned. Before the next decade was out (it
had even hardly begun!), there came along a
man to sum them both up, as far as regarded
novelty of matter or manner, and outdo them
quite. This man was Meyerbeer.

Wagner's sarcastic account of the matter was
received with outraged scorn when it first appeared, but is now seen to be substantially
true.

" Meyerbeer composed operas *à la* Rossini in
Italy only till the great wind began to veer
about in Paris, and Auber and Rossini blew the
new gale to a hurricane with the ' Muette' and
' Tell.' How soon Meyerbeer was in Paris! But
there he found, in the Gallicised Weber (remember ' *Robin des bois*') * and the be-Berliozed Beethoven, active forces which neither Auber nor

---

Robin des bois was what Berlioz quite rightly called an "in-
famous pasticcio" on Weber's *Freischütz*, cooked up by Castil-
Blaze, and brought out at the Odéon in Paris in 1824.

Rossini had noticed, as too far removed from
their purpose, but which he, with his all-the-
world's capacity, knew very well how to value
aright. He accordingly grasped together all
that thus offered itself to him into a mon-
strously variegated, composite phrase, before
the shrill outcry of which Auber and Rossini
suddenly became inaudible; the grim devil
'Robert' fetched them both together." *

Meyerbeer's genius has been variously estimated; forty or fifty years ago, it was rated
very high in France; now time has considerably tarnished its fabled brilliancy. But, whatever his genius, his influence upon the Opera,
not in France alone, but all over Europe, was
stronger and farther-reaching than that exerted by any other man in the nineteenth century,
save Richard Wagner. He alone can rank
with Lully and Gluck in having ushered in a
new epoch of French Grand Opera; of such
well-differentiated epochs French Grand Opera
as yet counts only three: the Lully, the Gluck,
and the Meyerbeer. To be sure, in comparing
him with Gluck, there is a certain notable
moral difference to be got over; Gluck was
essentially a reformer, a worshipper of eternal
Truth, while Meyerbeer was no reformer (in

* RICHARD WAGNER, *Gesammelte Schriften und Dichtungen*,
III., 364.

the Gluck sense) at all, and worshipped nothing but the everlasting Get-There.

Jakob Meyer Beer, known to the world as
Giacomo Meyerbeer, was born in Berlin on
September 5, 1791 (1794?), and died in Paris on
May 2, 1864. His father was a Jew, of the rich
banker sort. He studied under Franz Lauska,
Muzio Clementi, old Zelter (Mendelssohn's
master), and finally under the abbé Vogler.
As an opera-composer, he at first imitated
Weber, then (after studying vocal writing in
Italy, by Salieri's advice) took up with the extreme Rossini style; his *Crociato in Egitto* (Venice, 1824) may be called as good a reproduction
of the Rossini manner as exists. But his earlier operas (in his first and second manners)
are historically unimportant.

In 1826 he went to Paris.* Here he stopped
composing for a while, and began to make a
careful study of French literature and art,
above all, of the French character; these four
years, 1826–30, marked the turning-point in his
career. He was eminently a man of enterprise,
a born eclectic, unsurpassed in his faculty for
turning every opportunity to account; Paris
gave him food for thought. There were *La
muette* and *Guillaume Tell;* there was the new

---

* That is, before, not, as Wagner implies, after the production
of *La muette* and *Tell.*

Berlioz orchestration,— vehemently discussed
at the time, but descriable by the discerning eye
as big with a whole great future for the Art of
Music,—not yet applied to the Lyric Drama;
there were, in churches and conservatories, endless old contrapuntal subtleties, long neglected
by composers for the stage; best of all, there
was, as Wagner has said, a new wind blowing,
it was good weather for inventive audacity!

Meyerbeer plodded quietly on, catching idea
after idea, and silently perfecting a whole new
scheme of Opera; he was plainly not satisfied
until he had the plan complete in his brain,
well thought-out in every detail. For, when he
took to active composition again, we find his
third, or "grand," manner fully formed; he
had no transition period.

The work in which he embodied the results
of those four years of thinking and study was
Robert le Diable, brought out at the Académie
de Musique on November 21, 1831. The manner was quite new; a most composite style, if
you will, a mosaic style, made up of bits taken
from about every composer who had anything
worth taking, but—and here is the miracle!—
thoroughly personal and individual. No matter how great or how small a genius, there
was one force which Meyerbeer indisputably
possessed: the force of sharply defined indi-

MEYERBEER.

viduality; whencever he may have got an idea, once it had passed through his brain, it came out bearing his mark. No musical style was ever more composite than his; none more unmistakably the composer's own.

No doubt, other folk's ideas got more or less distorted in the process, and perverted from their original meaning. Often, what had been an irrepressible expression of a composer's inmost self was turned into a mere bid for effect. Meyerbeer was a man of no artistic conscience, and his artistic honesty was more than dubious; take him in the most charitable way, if Effect was really his god, he served that god with perfect single-heartedness.

Few operas have made so strong a first impression upon any public as *Robert le Diable* made in Paris in 1831. Success is not quite the word for it; *cela faisait explosion*, it made a tremendous noise in the world, was discussed, *pro* and *con*, with a vigour that left no one in doubt as to the work's being, at least, something! Whether great or puny, admirable or outrageous, it was clearly no nothing-at-all. The style was so new, and hence so incomprehensible at first, that everyone connected with the rehearsals — singers, players, conductor — predicted a flat failure. But, when the opening night came, the excitement of the audience

was so irrepressible and contagious that, after
the duet, "*Si j'aurai ce courage?*" in the third
act, Adolphe Nourrit, who sang the part of
Robert, lost head completely and, from sheer
madness of nervous tension, took a desperate
header down a trap-door that was open by
mistake—luckily falling upon a mattress, and
so saving his neck.*

It is difficult for us now to appreciate how
new *Robert* was in 1831. It seems old-fashioned
enough to-day! But look at the duet between
Alice and Bertram, "*Mais Alice, qu'as-tu donc?*"
in the third act, and think of what an audacity
of originality it took to offer those suppressed
intermittent whisperings, strung on the barest
thread of a melodic idea, to a public brought up
on Spontini, Cherubini, Auber, and Rossini! It
must have seemed the very impudence of crass,
unacademic realism. Take the unaccompanied
terzet, "*Fatal moment, cruel mystère,*" in the same
act, where a parody on the four-voice cadenza in
Beethoven's ninth symphony compelled a whole
public to applaud to the echo what, in Beethoven, they had scouted as incomprehensible.†

---

* The author has never seen this anecdote in print; it comes
orally from an eye-witness.

† At a rehearsal of the ninth symphony in Boston, some years
ago, a certain musician was overheard muttering, after the famous
quartet-cadenza, "There goes one of Meyerbeer's strongest claims
to *originality!*"

Robert is, after all, Meyerbeer's freshest and most original work. In *Les Huguenots* (1836) the style is more matured, there are moments of deeper inspiration—passages in the duet, "*O ciel! où courez-vous?*" between Raoul and Valentine, in the fourth act, have won sincere homage even from Wagner—but the first bloom is wiped off. In *Le Prophète* (1849) maturity of style already degenerates into mannerism; it out-Meyerbeers Meyerbeer. All that can be said of *L'Africaine*, his last opera (1864), is that, if no less mannered than the *Prophète*, it shows greater heartiness of inspiration. In *Robert le Diable* there is a superior freshness of melodic invention, more genuine dash and brilliancy.

With all his deplorable elasticity of artistic conscience, his flirting, now with grandeur, now with courtly elegance, and anon with downright vulgarity, Meyerbeer did the Opera no little good technical service. He loosened the bonds of musical form, and, though not quite obliterating the old landmarks, did much to render traditional forms more scenic. What most composers before him had done only in the act-finale he did at any point in an act where he saw a chance of making the music go hand in hand with a continuous dramatic development, no matter how brief. He obtained many of his dramatic and scenic results, to be sure, more by an extension than by a sacrifice of the old forms; but this was, after all, what most of his predecessors had done in the act-finale.

His style, composite as it was, was in the main essentially dramatic; nevertheless he did not discard the Rossini *coloratura*, over which his early Italian studies had given him a certain mastery. He was particularly fond of giving his second soprani—generally queens or princesses, of but secondary dramatic importance—intrinsically florid parts; his dramatic heroines, on the other hand, seldom have anything purely ornamental to sing, save in closing cadenzas; he seems to have felt that he could ill afford to withhold this concession to the vanity of singers.

Meyerbeer also did noteworthy work in *opéra-comique*, though he could never quite rid himself of a certain ponderousness, not wholly in accord with the genre. But nothing he did was in vain; and, if there had been no *Étoile du Nord* (1854) or *Pardon de Ploërmel* (1859), there surely would never have been a Bizet's *Carmen*.

In the last analysis, the Meyerbeer Opera was just as characteristic an expression of the romantic spirit of 1830 as Victor Hugo's and Dumas's dramas, Alfred de Musset's poetry, Delacroix's canvases, Berlioz's symphonies, or

Chopin's pianoforte-music. It was virtually
the Dumas Drama set to music,* and had all
the flaunting virtues and unnatural vices of that
school. If it was something very different from
the Wagnerian Music-Drama, this was simply
because nothing like the Wagnerian Music-
Drama could possibly have sprung from the
order of ideas which formed the point of
departure for the 1830 movement in France.
The most that can be expected of a tree is to
bear its own fruit!

Meyerbeer's chief follower was Jacques-
Fromenthal Halévy (1799–1862), a man of far
greater sincerity and warmth of feeling, but of
considerably less force. His reputation was
very high in his time, both in and out of France,
but only his *La Juive* (1835) remains on the active list to-day. †

---

* Eugène Scribe happens to have been Meyerbeer's librettist,
but that does not matter.

† Wagner tells a significant and instructive anecdote about *La
Juive* (the great Richard was a man of imagination, and one
never knows quite how far to trust him in matters of fact; but
this story bears all due internal evidence of truth). When Du-
prez was to succeed Nourrit in the part of Éléazar, he asked
Halévy one day at rehearsal if he might not hold back the tempo
a little in his great phrase, " *O ma fille chérie*," in the first finale,
as he found that he could make no effect with it at the general
tempo of the movement (*Allegro brillante*). Halévy willingly
granted his request; the news of this concession made by com-

The first native-born Frenchman, since Rameau, to win a higher reputation at the Académie de Musique than at the Opéra-Comique was Charles Gounod, born in Paris on June 17, 1818, died there on October 19, 1893. Formally and technically, he did nothing new ; in these matters he was purely and simply a follower of Meyerbeer, as none but the mightiest original genius could well have helped being in his time ; for the Meyerbeer cult in France from 1840 to 1880 was as general and enthusiastic as the Mendelssohn cult in England ; Meyerbeer ruled unquestioned and supreme. But Gounod did bring in a new personal temperament ; he was the great love-poet of the French lyric stage in the nineteenth century. Not particularly profound in feeling, but none the less genuine, well-nigh fanatical in his sincerity, he could mirror in his music all the dreamy ecstasy of a refined sensual passion—purely sensual, but thoroughly refined.

Gounod was really a one-work man, though box-office keepers may tell you another story ; all he really had to say he said in his *Faust* (first given at the Théâtre - Lyrique on March 19,

---

poser to singer was soon bruited abroad, with the result that, before long, this phrase was dragged out to a slow *Andante* in every opera-house in Europe. Many, if not most, operatic "traditions" have a very similar origin.

1859, then, after making the round of the world, at the Académie de Musique on March 3, 1869, as a grand opera, with added ballet in the fourth act). His other surviving opera, *Roméo et Juliette* (Académie de Musique, 1867), needs only to be compared with *Faust* to show the limitations of the man's genius. In a disconnected succession of dramatic situations, with few characters (*Faust*), he was completely at home; in a strenuously developed drama, like *Roméo et Juliette*, with multitudinous opportunities for drawing character, he was out of his element; out of his element, too, with the heavier orchestration demanded by the Académie de Musique—for remember, *Faust* was originally written for the smaller Théâtre-Lyrique. A small, tenuous voice, not devoid of a certain searching sweetness, Gounod has been listened to with delight for hard upon half a century; he even managed to make a sort of epoch of his own in a small way. But, save for his individual temperament, he left no mark upon the history of Opera; his formula was still the Meyerbeer formula, if somewhat relaxed—as formulæ have a way of relaxing, with the course of time. Gounod did not add a fourth to the trio of men who left the deepest impress on French Grand Opera: Lully, Gluck, and Meyerbeer.

VII

The Germans

EIGHTEEN years after the production of Mozart's *Don Giovanni* in Prag, there came in Vienna another notable first performance: that of Beethoven's *Fidelio* at the Theater an der Wien on November 20, 1805.

If Beethoven (1770–1827) wrote only one opera, he was clearly determined that that one should be a lion! Probably no other opera in the whole list was ever so worked over by its composer as this *Fidelio, oder die eheliche Liebe*.

The text was originally adapted by Joseph Sonnleithner from Jean-Nicolas Bouilly's *Léonore, ou l'amour conjugal*, which had been twice set to music: first, in the original French, by Pierre Gaveaux (1761–1825), and brought out at the Feydeau in Paris on February 19, 1798; then in an Italian translation, by Ferdinando Paër (1771–1839), and given in Dresden on October 3, 1804. By no means a great text, of eternal significance, like that of *Don Giovanni,*

but a mere bit of sentimental-heroic Melodrama, thoroughly bourgeois, a play for mon-
sieur Poirrier to weep delicious tears over.
The best that can be said of it is that it is good
of its kind.

As at first given, Beethoven's opera was in
three acts, the overture being the one generally known as the "*Leonore* No. 2"; it was
withdrawn after three performances. The libretto was next given to Stephen Breuning to
work over; he reduced it to two acts, and the
opera was given in this remodelled shape, with
a new overture, known as the "*Leonore* No. 3,"
at the Imperial Privat-Theater on March 29,
1806; it was again withdrawn, after two performances. There was some talk of giving the
opera in Prag in 1807, and Beethoven wrote the
overture known as the "*Leonore* No. 1" for the
purpose; but the plan came to nothing. At
last the libretto was given to Friedrich Treitsch-
ke for a second revision, Beethoven also re-
modelling his score; in this final shape the
opera was given, with the overture known
as "to *Fidelio*" (in E major), at the Kärnthnerthor-Theater on May 13, 1814.

Fidelio was the second great opera in the
form of the German *Singspiel* (that is, with
spoken dialogue), Mozart's *Zauberflöte* being the
first. If Beethoven showed little distinction of

taste in his choice of libretto, he certainly made up for it in his treatment; *Fidelio* is unquestionably the greatest German opera between Mozart and Wagner. It is as idle to compare the music with that of *Don Giovanni*—though this has too often been foolishly done—as to compare the two libretti. *Fidelio* is as thoroughly German as *Don Giovanni* is Italian. But its falling short of the *Don Giovanni* mark is chiefly owing to the composer's well-nigh fanatical fidelity to his libretto: of that unvarying level of the highest sort of *opera buffa*, suddenly rising at the close to the sublimest heights of Lyric Tragedy, which characterizes Mozart's masterpiece, we find nothing; Beethoven lets, not only his expression, but his very style follow the text, step by step; the music accordingly keeps oscillating between good, comfortable *opéra-comique* and the most impassioned tragedy — for, when the strenuous moments come, Beethoven takes his melodramatic text quite seriously, and writes music on a level with any greatest lines you please in Æschylus, Sophocles, or Shakspere. Then, at the end, when all is over, he suddenly throws off the stage shackles—really shackles to him, as they never were to Mozart—and launches out into a jubilant cantata (you can call it nothing else, it can not be acted to) in the ninth symphony vein,* as if fairly drunk with the joy of being once more on his own ground.

It is in its music, and in that alone, that *Fidelio* is great; and, compared with the exquisite finish of vocal and orchestral writing in *Don Giovanni*, this music is as if hewn out with a broad-axe. Of Mozart's admirable science in writing for the human voice Beethoven had little; he is known to have said once: "Singers ought to be able to do anything, except bite their own noses!" But, in spite of its lack of homogeneity of style, there is not a moment in the music that is not great in its way; for one thing, the outburst, "*Es schlägt der Rache Stunde*," near the close of the "Pistol"-quartet in the second act (after the trumpet-calls), is probably the most overwhelming moment of sheer unbridled fury in all Opera. When it came to passion, Beethoven could make the best of them look small. With all its shortcomings, this uncouth cub of a *Fidelio* is still a lion!

It is, after all, only because of its intrinsic greatness that *Fidelio* has any historical importance; there was nothing new in it, save

---

*The librettist has even paraphrased the lines, "*Wer ein holdes Weib errungen, mische seinen Jubel ein!*" in Schiller's *Ode an die Freude*,—which Beethoven afterwards set in his ninth symphony,—changing them to "*Wer ein holdes Weib errungen, stimm' in unsern Jubel ein.*"

the Beethoven temperament; it marks no epoch. It is only eternal.

But something new was soon to come; the German Romantic Movement was in the wind. This new departure in German Music, and especially in German Opera, should not be confounded with the so-called movement of 1830 in France. This latter, which embraced all the fine arts and *belles-lettres* generally, was, in the last analysis, a revolt against the classic; not only against the formal principles of classic Art, but against well-nigh all classic artistic habitudes and points of view. For the Renaissance revival of the Antique, it substituted a modern revamping of the Middle Ages; the traditional themes of the Drama, in particular, were transformed, and its ethical gist, as Nietzsche would say, transvalued. The inexorableness of Fate could, to be sure, hardly die out as a dramatic mainspring; but Patriotism and Duty—after Fate, the most important themes of the classic Drama — were superseded by Passion.

Of all this, little is to be found in the German romantic Opera; in Germany the Romantic Movement meant merely a discarding of traditional tragico-heroic subjects in favour of subjects taken from national, or even local, folklore. Practically the most conspicuous item in it all was the prominent part played by the supernatural element; without the supernatural, folk-lore is no longer folk-lore!

The heads of the new romantic school were Weber and Spohr.*

Louis Spohr was born in Brunswick on April 5, 1784, and died in Cassel on November 22, 1859. With his reputation as a great master of the violin we have nothing to do here; he interests us simply as an opera-composer, and, in this field, his reputation equalled any in Germany in his time. After writing three operas which were still-born, he brought out *Der Zweikamph mit der Geliebten* in Hamburg in 1811. Of his eleven operas, *Faust* (1818) and *Jessonda* (1823) are the most famous; his last, *Die Kreuzfahrer*, was given in Cassel in 1845.

Karl Maria, Freiherr von Weber, was born at Eutin in the grand-duchy of Oldenburg on December 18, 1786, and died in London on June 5, 1826.† After passing from one teacher

---

* Weber was, at first, unhesitatingly credited with originating the movement; later, this credit was given to Spohr, because his *Faust* (produced in 1818) antedated Weber's *Freischütz* (1821). But this specious argument is stultified by the fact that, though Spohr's *Faust* was completed five years before its production (that is, in 1813), Weber had written his *Rübezahl* (unfinished and never brought out) for a theatre in Breslau as early as 1806.

† It has already been mentioned that Weber was first cousin to Mozart's wife; it may also be of interest that, with the exception

to another (Michael Haydn was among them), he, like Meyerbeer, completed his musical studies under the abbé Vogler. After writing (more or less completely) three operas which never saw the foot-lights, he brought out his *Sylvana* in Frankfort-on-the-Main in 1810—a year before Spohr's *Zweikampf*. But his reputation could not fairly be called national before the production of *Der Freischütz* in Berlin in 1821, and its subsequent triumphal progress all over Germany. This was followed by *Euryanthe* (Vienna, 1823) and *Oberon* (London, 1826).

Der Freischütz was in every sense an epoch-making work ; it marked the first unquestionable victory scored by the new romantic school. To understand the impression it produced in Germany, we must appreciate what had been the operatic conditions in that country when Weber and Spohr came upon the scene, and what those conditions were in their day.

Up to the close of the eighteenth century, native operatic production in Germany was in

---

of the Bachs, he had the longest musical pedigree of any noteworthy composer on record. Philipp Emanuel Bach and his brothers belonged to the fifth consecutive generation of professional musicians in the direct line of descent. Karl Maria von Weber belonged to the fourth generation of musicians in his family—the first two of these being, however, represented by amateurs.

much the same case as in France: it had only one foreign rival to compete with, the imported Italian article. But the difficulty of this competition was far more serious in Germany than in France; the Italian composers who came to Germany did not turn German in their music, as Gluck, Cherubini, Spontini, Rossini, and others turned French in Paris; and, with the beginning of the new century, a fresh set of rivals sprang up—the French themselves. The importation of French operas began, while that of Italian operas in no wise diminished.

Among a host of more or less important foreign names may be mentioned Ferdinando Paër (1771–1839),* who, as court Kapellmeister to the Elector of Saxony, ruled over the Hofoper in Dresden from 1801 to 1806; Cherubini (who, though Italian by birth, must count as half-German, half-French as a composer) was in Vienna from 1805 to 1808, where his *Faniska* (Kärnthnerthor-Theater, 1806) made such a success that it was deemed excessive praise to Beethoven's *Fidelio* to predict, as someone did, that, one day, it would " rank as high as Cherubini's *Faniska*," and Beethoven himself recognized Cherubini as the leading opera-composer of the day. Spontini was called in 1820 to the

---

* He Teutonized himself to the extent of signing his name " Pär " while in Germany.

Hofoper in Berlin, and brought his *Vestale* and *Cortez* with him.* Beside the personal presence of these crowned representatives of the Académie de Musique and the Opéra-Comique, the importation of French operas soon began to assume very considerable dimensions. What with having to compete with both Italians and French, — and in vernacular translations, too, to be understood by the vulgar, — German composers were hard put to it.

There was nothing to offend or unsettle German habits in the French *opéra-comique*, for its form (with spoken dialogue) was the same as that of the native *Spieloper*. This was not quite true of Italian Opera, when sung in the original tongue; but the Germans adapted both the *opera seria* and the *opera buffa* to their taste easily enough in translated versions, by substituting spoken dialogue for the "unaccompanied" *recitativo secco*. But French Grand Opera—in which all the recitative was of the "accompanied" sort, for which no spoken dialogue could be substituted with any semblance of fidelity to the original—was a new and unaccustomed form to the German public; for the

---

* The operas he wrote especially for Berlin—*Nurmahal, oder das Rosenfest zu Kaschmir* (1822) and *Agnes von Hohenstauffen* (1829)—fall after the Weber period—at least, after his death.

old Keiser school was long since a thing of the past, and forgotten. An opera in which everything was sung presented a new problem for German perspicacity to struggle with ; for, whether naturally gifted with a keen dramatic sense or not, this public had formed the habit of at least wishing to understand what it heard in the vernacular, and singing was not favourable to easy comprehension.* It is probably owing to this insatiate thirst for understanding on the part of the public that the form of the German *Spieloper* was as long-lived as it was; a form bastard in itself, and especially, even ludicrously unfit for the treatment of heroic or highly poetic subjects. In France it never rose higher than the *opéra-comique*.

This unfitness—which seems to have escaped Mozart's perception completely, as it did also Beethoven's—was felt keenly by both Spohr and Weber, especially as they had the better French example under their very noses — in

---

* It is characteristic at once of German economy and of the German desire to understand things that the opera-libretti published in Germany (for the benefit of opera-goers) contain, as a rule, only the text of the musical numbers and recitatives, but not that of the spoken dialogue—which everyone is expected to understand without following, book in hand. The standard formula on the title-page is, not the title of the opera, as with us, but "*Lieder und Gesänge aus* (Songs and Vocal Pieces from)" whatever the opera may be.

Gluck's operas and others still more French. No doubt the *Freischütz* owed part of its success to its *Spieloper* form ; Weber's genius, the homelike quality of the legend on which the text was based, the general sylvan atmosphere of both text and music,* were also for much in this success ; but it was nevertheless the putting of these familiar things in the familiar way that unfailingly brought the work home to the popular heart. Still, Weber was not blind to the imperfection of the form. Both he and Spohr, apparently without collusion, determined to remedy it. In the year 1823 were brought out the first two entirely "*durchcomponierte*" (set to music all through) German operas since Keiser : Spohr's *Jessonda*, in Cassel on July 28, and Weber's *Euryanthe*, in Vienna on October 25.† Neither experiment was a success with the public, who, though willing enough to forgive that sort of thing in foreign operas (as an irremediable product of Gallic perverseness), kicked lustily against it in a work of native growth.

This matter of recitative *vs.* spoken dialogue was really of no small importance ; and it is highly probable that the German objection to

---

* The average German can be brought to the verge of tears by the mere mention of the word *Wald !*

† Here, at least, Spohr has the priority—by three months !

giving up the latter was not based solely upon its being more easily understood by the listener. To go to the root of the business, we must remember that the so-called "accompanied" recitative (*recitativo stromentato*) was a common property of every form of Opera,—in Italy, France, and Germany,—whereas the *recitativo secco* was purely Italian. The Italians were the only people who had devised an appropriate style for the musical setting of familiar, colloquial dialogue; and this style was the rapid, flexible *recitativo quasi-parlando* (or almost spoken recitative), which was free from all restraint from musical rhythm, and had become, by long convention, less bound by considerations of tonality than any other known form of composition.* In the delivery of this sort of recitative, rhythm and emphasis depended solely upon the rhetorical sense of the text, the singer was free to use the same *diction* (as the French say) that he would in ordinary speech. The accompanied recitative, on the other hand, was a much more heroic business; all opera-writing nations seem to have agreed, as by common consent, that it was applicable only in

---

* It is significant that, as far back as Handel, one seldom finds any "signature" (indication of key) at the beginning of a *secco* recitative; the composer set out with the expectation of changing key frequently and at short notice.

the " grand style "; there was nothing colloquial about it.

The (real or supposed) incompatibility of the
French and German languages with anything
like the Italian *recitativo parlando*—which, after
all, only carried the natural sing-song of South-
Italian (Neapolitan or Sicilian) speech an inch
farther in the musical direction—was one of the
reasons why the French took to the make-shift
of spoken dialogue in their *opéra-comique*, and
the Germans, in every sort of Opera. Both
felt that there were many situations in Opera
where the more magniloquent accompanied
recitative would be out of place ; and for the
homelier Italian form they could find no better
substitute than bare spoken dialogue. Moreover, as time wore on, and traditions crystallized
into habits, French and German singers, having
had to do only with accompanied recitative, got
to associate a certain grandiosity of manner
with every sort of musically set dialogue or
monologue ; so that, had composers sought to
introduce a more colloquial style, there would
have been little chance of their having it fitly
sung.*

* Particularly instructive on this head is what Berlioz writes
about his experience with the recitatives he had written to take
the place of the spoken dialogue in Weber's *Der Freischütz*, for
the production of that opera in French, under his direction, at the

Now, the German public, being accustomed to have nearly all the important part of the story of the opera told them in (generally rather homely) spoken dialogue, naturally resented having it told them in stately recitative, which, beside rendering the text less easy to understand, was often too evidently grandiosely out of place, and took up an unwarrantable amount of time. For neither Spohr nor Weber gave them anything corresponding to the Italian *parlando*, but followed the more orotund French model.

Still other causes, too, militated against the experiment's being accepted as successful. Spohr, with all his virtues, was not a genius of the epoch-making sort, not a man to shake the

---

Académie de Musique in 1841—spoken dialogue being against the rules of the house. "I never could get the singers to abandon their slow, heavy, bombastic way of singing recitative; especially in the scenes between Max and Caspar did their delivery of the essentially simple and familiar conversation have all the pomp and solemnity of a scene of Lyric Tragedy." (*Mémoires*, 328.)

Wagner (*Ges. Schr. u. Dicht.*, I., 287) writes of this performance: "The way in which the recitatives were *sung* increased in no small degree the weight of blame cast upon them; all the singers thought to have to do with *Norma* or *Moses*, they brought in throughout *portamenti*, *tremolo*-nuances, and such like noble things."

These recitatives of Berlioz's, by the way, were probably the first attempt at doing anything colloquial in that line in French.

world out of old habits; and Weber, who certainly was, had the ill luck to find, in *Euryanthe*, about the most deplorable libretto that can be imagined. If Mozart's music could float *Die Zauberflöte*, Weber's certainly could not float *Euryanthe*; the self-complacent Helmine von Chézy had hardly put worse balderdash upon paper when she cooked up the book of *Rosamunde*, in five days, for Franz Schubert. Neither was the text the only trouble; Weber betrayed something of the 'prentice hand in his recitatives, he did not fall easily and naturally into the vein, and gave little evidence of that dramatic power which he showed in his grand *scenas* in the *Freischütz* and *Oberon*. The best that can be said of his experiment is that it was a well-meant, if rather blundering, move in an artistic direction.

But, if, in this instance, the will was somewhat better than the deed, Weber's service to Opera in other ways was none the less conspicuous. He brought — as Cavalli did before him, in Venice, if not quite in the same way—the popular element into serious Opera, and the form itself closer to the hearts of the German people. This Mozart, one of the most intrinsically aristocratic geniuses in all Music, had never done; neither had Beethoven—notwithstanding the bourgeois quality of the *Fidelio*-text

—done it much more than he. But in Weber's melody, no matter how broad in style or elaborately ornamented, you get all the romantic, out-of-door freshness of the Suabian folk-song, the peculiarly Teutonic sentimentality in its best expression ; one might almost say he wrote in dialect. And if, in this, he did the Opera good service in Germany, he did other things, of a technical sort, the influence of which was farther-reaching. He effected a sort of interweaving of the *scena* * with the aria that did much to relax strictness of conventional form, and rendered the form more scenically plastic. The so-called Incantation-scene in the *Freischütz* even reaches out toward the Wagnerian Music-Drama, almost as much as the Statue-scene in *Don Giovanni*. It positively terrified contemporary pedants ; but, when someone

---

* The term *scena* is applied to an accompanied recitative of more than usual length and dramatic quality, often (but not necessarily) containing passages in the *arioso* style. Donna Anna's recitative " *Era già alquanto avanzata la notte*," which debouches into the aria, " *Or sai chi l'onore*," in the first act of *Don Giovanni*, is a transcendent example of the older form of scena. Leonore's " *Ascheulicher ! wo eilst du hin ?* " in *Fidelio*, is another. Of Weber's intermingling of the scena with the aria, Max's " *Nein ! länger trag' ich nicht die Qualen*," and Agathe's " *Nie nahte mir der Schlummer*," in *Der Freischütz*, and Rezia's "Ocean ! thou mighty monster," in *Oberon*, are conspicuous examples.

showed it to Beethoven, that appreciative great man said : " If the scene was to be set to music, I don't see how it could have been done in any other way." In this scene Weber shows all his romantic deviltry ; probably no other composer in the whole list ever supped with the Devil with so short a spoon. Upon the whole, the supernatural was an element very congenial to him ; few composers have treated it so to the manner born, with so little of the melodramatic, as he. The fairy music in *Oberon* stands unapproached ; well might Wagner exclaim : " Compared with those fairies, Mendelssohn's * are, at best, *flies !* " As a mere matter of record, perhaps not uninteresting as such to Anglo-Saxons, be it said that Weber, the German, wrote the only modern English opera that can in any way stand in the first class : *Oberon ; or, The Elf-King's Oath* (to a text by James R. Planché, brought out at Covent Garden in London on April 12, 1826, not two months before the composer's death).

It is, after all, more by his interweaving of the *scena* with the aria than by his banishing spoken dialogue that Weber did the best service to the Opera in Germany, and elsewhere. In this dramatic extension of the aria—and of cognate ensemble forms—he was most especially

---

* In *A Midsummer Night's Dream.*

WEBER.

imitated by Meyerbeer in France; indeed, this sort of thing was one of the chief items in the Meyerbeer formula.

If *Euryanthe*, in spite of much admirable music, was a failure, *Der Freischütz* was surely not; it made an epoch in German Opera, and imitators were not wanting. Among Weber's followers, two are important: Heinrich Marschner (1796–1861) and Peter von Lindpaintner (1791–1856). These were men of a certain amount of genius; though their works hardly crossed the German frontier, they held the stage long and prosperously throughout Germany; their operas were not mere "*Kapellmeister* work." Marschner was decidedly the stronger of the two; his *Der Vampyr* (Leipzig, 1828), *Der Templer und die Jüdin* (the libretto after Scott's *Ivanhoe;* ib., 1829), and especially his masterpiece, *Hans Heiling* (Berlin, 1833), must rank not far below Weber's operas. Lindpaintner's talent was of a more ordinary, showier cast; his best-known works are *Der Vampyr* (Vienna, 1829) and *Lichtenstein* (the text after Wilhelm Hauff's novel; Stuttgart, 1846).*

---

* In a book like the present, many a subject of secondary importance must perforce be treated summarily; such a subject is the German comic Opera, or *Singspiel*. Although filling quite an enormous place in the national artistic life, it has been absolutely

without influence upon anything outside of Germany, or upon the higher forms of classic and romantic Opera in Germany itself. With the exception of Mozart's thrice-admirable *Entführung aus dem Serail* (Vienna, 1782), Otto Nicolai's *Die lustigen Weiber von Windsor* (Berlin, 1849), and Ignaz Brüll's *Das goldene Kreuz* (ib., 1875), exceedingly few works of this order are known outside of Germany; most of the older ones of the school have passed into the antique-curiosity stage, and are more than dead now.

Let the following list of composers and characteristic operas do duty for anything further on the subject:

Josef Haydn (1732–1809), *Der neue krumme Teufel* (Vienna, 1752); Johann Adam Hiller (1728–1804), *Der Teufel ist los* (Leipzig, 1766), *Der Dorfbarbier, Die Jagd* (ib., 1772); Karl Ditters von Dittersdorf (1739–1799), *Doktor und Apotheker* (Vienna, 1786); Johann Friedrich Reichardt (1752–1814), *Hänschen und Gretchen* (Königsberg, 1772), *Das Zauberschloss* (Berlin, 1802); Peter von Winter (1754–1825), *Das unterbrochene Opferfest* (Vienna, 1796); Joseph Weigl (1766–1846), *Die Schweizerfamilie* (Vienna, 1809); Konradin Kreutzer (1780–1849), *Jery und Bäthely* (Vienna, 1810), *Das Nachtlager in Granada* (ib., 1834); Franz Schubert (1797–1828), *Der häusliche Krieg* (Vienna, 1861); Albert Lortzing (1803–1851), *Czar und Zimmermann* (Leipzig, 1837), *Der Wildschütz* (ib., 1843), *Der Waffenschmied zu Worms* (Vienna, 1846); Ignaz Brüll (1846—still living), *Das steinerne Herz* (text after Hauff; Prag, 1888).

VIII

Wagner

AFTER Scarlatti and Handel, Gluck; after Donizetti and Meyerbeer, Wagner—born in Leipzig on May 22, 1813, died in Venice on February 13, 1883.

He began as anything but a reformer; his first viable opera, *Rienzi* (brought out in Dresden in 1842), was nothing but an Académie de Musique grand opera in five acts. Indeed, it was written especially for the great Paris house, though never accepted there; and the style of its music is closely modelled upon that of the then reigning Grand Opera favourites in France: Spontini, Meyerbeer, and Donizetti.*

---

* Donizetti's *Les martyrs* and *La favorite* were produced at the Académie de Musique in 1840; the latter is still in the repertory to this day.

Wagner's two earlier operas—*Die Feen* (written in 1833, but only brought out posthumously in Munich in 1888) and *Das Liebesverbot* (Magdeburg, 1836)—have no historical importance. A certain biographical importance they surely have, if only in showing how unsettled Wagner's artistic convictions were in his youth; *Das Liebesverbot* is written mainly in imitation of Bellini—of all men in the world!

It is virtually a Meyerbeer grand opera, written with more sincerity, full of youthful excessiveness in every direction, but lacking the highly-developed Meyerbeer technique. It was Wagner's first and last work of the sort.

In his next opera, *Der fliegende Holländer* (Dresden, 1843), he quite abandoned the French model, and turned back to Germany and Weber. To be sure, he gave up spoken dialogue,—a far safer experiment in the 'forties than in the 'twenties,—but, if there had never been a *Freischütz*, there never would have been a *Holländer*. Yet, notwithstanding the strong Weberish streak in this opera,* there is less homogeneity of style in the music than in any other of Wagner's works; beside the Weber influence, there is, at times, distinctly that of French *opéra-comique*.† All these borrowings are, however, recognizably coloured with Wagner's own individuality; now and then you

---

* There is an almost perplexing variety of Weber in it: Weber very nearly pure and simple, only slightly Wagnerized; Weber Spontinified and Meyerbeerized (Senta's and Holländer's duet, "*Wie aus der Ferne längst vergang'ner Zeiten*," in the second act); Weber Donizettified (Erik's cavatina, "*Willst jenes Tag's du nicht dich mehr entsinnen?*"); and what not else.

† The spinning chorus, the chattering little chorus of girls, "*Sie sind daheim!*" and, above all, Daland's air, "*Mögst du, mein Kind*,"—which last may be described as indifferent good Méhul.

even get Wagner pure and simple.* Technically speaking, the musical forms are very
considerably relaxed; more, upon the whole,
than in any opera of Meyerbeer's. The separate numbers are often, so to speak, ravelled out
at the ends, that they may be woven together
into some semblance of a continuous whole;
only a semblance as yet, but Wagner is plainly
coming to himself.

He took a good while to do it, though; in
his next opera, *Tannhäuser und der Sänger-
krieg auf Wartburg* (Dresden, 1845), he makes a
new experimental throw of the dice. Wagner
was essentially a man of vast ideas, most comfortably at home in "large frames," as the
French say. In *Tannhäuser* we have what is
intrinsically a romantic opera masquerading
in the guise of Grand Opera; although only in
three acts, it is on the largest French scale.
Shortly before his death, Wagner called it:
"*meine schlechtste Oper* (my worst opera)"; and
not wholly without justice. The musical style
is more homogeneous than in the *Holländer*,
but Weber still stands largely in the fore-

---

* Notably in Senta's ballad, "*Traft ihr das Schiff im Meere
an?*"—though with the last outburst (*Allegro con fuoco*), "*Ich
sei 's, die dich durch ihre Treu' erlöse!*" Weber stands out more
prominently than ever. A comparison of this passage with
Agathe's "*All' meine Pulse schlagen*," in *Der Freischütz*, will
leave no doubt on this head.

ground. A most strangely transmogrified
Weber, however: at times pretty thoroughly
Wagnerized,* but, for the most part, washed
over with a coat of the most bourgeois sort of
German thoosy-moosy, redolent of the merely
Bänkelsänger spirit of men like Franz Abt and
F. W. Kücken! Never before nor since did
Wagner strike so essentially vulgar a vein of
melody. What saves *Tannhäuser* is the beauty of the story, the complete sincerity of the
music, and Wagner's unerring dramatic touch
—which last he had by nature. The technique,
however, is still rather feeble, except in the
matter of a skilful handling of material means—
the orchestra and choral masses; the score is
defaced by some mere school-boy clumsinesses,
which were called Wagnerish at the time, but
are now seen to be anything but that. Yet in
Tannhäuser we do descry at times the beginning
of Wagner's third manner;† developed with

---

* As in Tannhäuser's song to Venus, and in one or two of the
songs in the Singing-Contest (Walther's and two of Tannhäuser's).

† Especially in Tannhäuser's Narrative, "*Inbrunst im Herzen*,"
in the third act, and all the ensuing struggle between him and
Wolfram before the opened Venus Mountain. Remember, by the
way, that the now authorized "Paris" version of the first Bac-
chanale and the scene between Tannhäuser and Venus was written
some fifteen or sixteen years later (after *Tristan*) and is no crite-
rion of the style of the original opera.

no very conspicuous technical skill, but already wiping out all traditional musical forms; here the plastic form of the music is based upon nothing but the dramatic development of the scene.

With *Lohengrin* (Weimar, 1850) comes a magnificent change. It is still romantic Opera parading as Grand Opera; but of the Abt-Kücken melodic *roture* there is no longer a trace; the musical style is distinction itself. Weber almost disappears; what there is left of him is no more than the little occasional touch of Haydn to be found in the works of Beethoven's second period. For the first time, Wagner succeeds in raising his music to the full level of his poetic conception; the vehicle is worthy of the load!* The third manner crops up, too, in a far more developed condition in the opening scene of the second act (Ortrud and Telramund on the church steps by night). *Lohengrin* was em-

---

* The score of *Lohengrin* is, in one particular, an interesting commentary on the absolute naïveté of Wagner's mental attitude toward old conventions. A convention was never bad in his eyes because it was conventional, but merely because it was intrinsically bad. One of the old fashions most laughed at by the come-outers of Wagner's time—by Berlioz, Liszt, and himself—was the frequently recurring perfect authentic cadence. Yet *Lohengrin* may be called a very apotheosis of the perfect cadence; there are nearly as many perfect cadences in it as in a Handel oratorio, or an opera by Cimarosa.

phatically Wagner's transition opera; after it, he left the "Opera" entirely for the Music-Drama.

It was *Lohengrin* that fully opened Wagner's eyes to what he wanted. And, now that we have followed him so far in his career, we can see how very purblind his vision in this matter had been. Taking the ground, both by instinct and rational conviction, that the Opera must be primarily a form of Drama, and only secondarily a form of Music, he was some time in discovering the way in which he personally could best make it a worthy form of Drama; *Rienzi*, the *Holländer*, *Tannhäuser*, and *Lohengrin* were but experiments to this end, and experiments, too, guided by no particularly definite theoretical hypothesis.*

* One point in all these operas is exceedingly hard to explain, unless it be explicable by the strong hold convention and example still had upon Wagner. He wrote all his own libretti, and so could not fall back upon his text as an excuse for any dramatic shortcoming. It is accordingly very curious that, even up to *Lohengrin*, he should so frequently have followed one of the least commendable Italian examples: in what may be called the de-dramatization of the act-finale. In Rossini, Donizetti, Bellini, and the younger Verdi is often to be found a most signal falling-off from the high standard set by Mozart in this matter. Instead of that extended period of continuous dramatic development which we find, say, in both the finales in *Don Giovanni*, these Italians give us, for the most part, act-finales built on the aria plan: consisting, after some essentially dramatic preluding, of a concerted

But between the productions of *Tannhäuser*
and *Lohengrin* came his exile, for participating
in the revolutionary business of 1848, and flight
to Switzerland. Here he had leisure to think,
to account to himself for those artistic instincts
for which he had hitherto found no adequate
form of expression, and to formulate his theory
of the Music-Drama. In this period fall the
writing and publication of *Das Kunstwerk der
Zukunft* and *Oper und Drama*, his principal
theoretico-controversial works. But what best
helped to open his eyes was what he had done,
and left undone, in writing *Lohengrin*.

What his opened eyes saw clearly was, up-

slow movement, followed by a quick one, with just enough dramatic business intervening, logically to explain the change of
tempo. It is like the confidante's consolatory philosophical reflec-
tions after the prima donna's *cavatina*, that give her the desired cue
for her *cabaletta*. During neither slow movement nor *stretto* does
anything dramatic happen ; these two movements are intrinsically
nothing but concert-pieces sung in costume. Now, for just this
undramatic sort of act-finale Wagner shows a considerable fondness in his "operas." Characteristic instances are the second
finale in *Rienzi*, the first and second in *Tannhäuser*, and the first
in *Lohengrin*. He does this sort of thing decidedly oftener than
Meyerbeer. To be sure, he also follows the better Mozart model
—say, in the fourth and fifth finales in *Rienzi*, the third in both
Tannhäuser and *Lohengrin*—and even his undramatic finales can
not truly be said to be "out of situation"; they are amply justified
by the text. But it seems nevertheless strange that a man of his
dramatic aspirations should have given himself the opportunities
he did to write them at all.

on the whole, this.* Ever since Marc' Antonio
Cesti, emulating his master Carissimi's exploits,
had driven the operatic chariot into that Oratorio no-thoroughfare (in Venice, about 1649), no
composer had had the radical insight and skill
to back the hapless vehicle out again. Man
after man had sprung to the horses' heads and
tried to turn them back, to make an exit in that
dignified fashion. But there was not room
enough to turn round in; there the chariot
stood, a stone wall across the end of the pole,
musical haberdashery shops on either side, advance and retrogression alike impracticable;
for, with the heavy load accumulated while in
the *cul-de-sac*, backing was out of the question.
Then came Gluck, who, after lightening the
load a bit,—throwing out ornamental frippery,
four-times-repeated words, needless *ritornelli*,
and the like,—gave such a sturdy tug at the
reins that his team really did back—half-way
out; but there he stuck fast. The Opera still
remained virtually what Cesti had made it: not
a Drama with auxiliary Music, but *a Dramma
per musica*—a Drama for (the sake of) Music.

Wagner was the first to see clearly what the
true state of the case was : that there was nothing for it but to throw out the whole load that

* It may be as well to say at once that this is the author's, not
Wagner's own, statement of the case.

had been accumulated during two centuries' lingering in that hopeless no-thoroughfare— all, save one thing alone!—and then back the lightened chariot the whole way out. Throw to the four winds of Orcus well-nigh all that had been gained in two centuries, and start afresh on the open highway—from what point, think you? From precisely the point whence the Florentine *Camerata* and Peri and Caccini had set out in 1595. With this important difference, however: whereas Caccini and Peri had the whole Art of Music lying before them in the problematical condition of a new-made *tabula rasa*, with no technique at their beck at all adequate to grapple with the problem, Wagner had a whole two centuries' development of technique ready-made to his hand—which technique, moreover, he purposed considerably augmenting for his own behoof. The Wagner Reform was, as Carlyle said of the French Revolution, a sudden return to primordial conditions, but with all the appliances of civilization.

When it takes a book of over four hundred pages to expound a theory of the Music-Drama, that theory is not easily epitomized in a few paragraphs. Yet the task is not quite so impracticable as it looks. *Oper und Drama*, Wagner's theoretical *magnum opus*, is full of

redundancies, of poetico-philosophical specula-
tions, hair-splitting meticulosities, and hazy
dreams. With due insight for a reagent, an
enormous mass of useless matter can be pre-
cipitated out from it, leaving a clear solution of
artistic principles, not over-hard to deal with.
Upon the whole, *Oper und Drama* is the work of
a man who had not got over the first splenetic
teeth-gnashing at his exile, who, for the first
time in his life, had set himself to think out his
problem to the bitter end, and, being by nature
more poet than philosopher, had the nimblest
faculty for taking pregnant hints from everything that caught his notice, and that un-
quenchable, naïf enthusiasm which impels the
amateur logician to swear by every wildest de-
duction he may have drawn from his premises.
Wagner gave ample evidence, in after life, of
how little finality he imputed to his *Oper und
Drama ;* the book really marks but one stage
in his mental and artistic growth, and takes
points of view which he considerably outgrew
later.*

---

* Compare, for instance, the dogged obstinacy with which he in-
sists, in *Oper und Drama*, upon the popular Myth, or Legend,
being the only fit material for a drama, with the frank ebulliency
of his reply (at Bayreuth, in 1882, the first *Parsifal* year) to a certain musician who had expressed a preference for his *Meistersinger* over all his other works: "Yes!" cried he, "you may be

Stripped of its dialectic trappings, and with its metaphysical convolutions straightened out, Wagner's theory is briefly this. In any sort of Drama, whether musical or otherwise, the play's the thing; and, in the Music-Drama, the music must lend itself unreservedly and continuously to intensifying the emotional ex-

---

right, there; you see, the *Meistersinger* was, after all, an inspiration, it came straight out of the blue; no rummaging about among musty old myths was needed to make that!"

Again, as a fair example of the amateurish futility of much of his reasoning, take his theory of the Supernatural in the Drama. His argument (much condensed) is this. In real life, every act of ours is the result of a well-nigh endless chain of causes, and is hence not thoroughly comprehensible until all these causes and their interconnection are known. For setting forth such a causal chain—to explain the actions of his *dramatis personæ*—the dramatist has no time; the novelist can do it, but the dramatist can not. Yet a work of art must be able to make itself understood immediately and through and through; nothing in it must seem unaccountable. So the dramatist has to condense the whole chain of hidden causes into one immediately visible and comprehensible cause, which, from this very process of potentization, must needs appear as supernatural. An excellent explanation of the function of the Supernatural in the Drama, if you will; but so utterly needless! Everyone in his senses knows, unless he be an impenitent realist, that the Supernatural (in modern romantic Drama, at least) is always symbolical; and most of us are perfectly ready to recognize its symbolism. But Wagner, who, with all his romanticism, was a pretty hard-and-fast realist at bottom, could not rest content with his equally inborn fondness for the Supernatural until he had argued himself into the paradox of recognizing it as a *realistic necessity*.

pression of the text, and to giving an illustrative colouring to the dramatic action. In the end,—aye, and even down to minute details,—it is the theory of the old Florentine *Camerata*, and nothing else under the sun.

As to the practical means by which Music can best fulfil this its allotted mission, two points in Wagner's theory are noteworthy; the first fundamental, the second more adventitious. The first point is that Music must abandon all those forms which were developed, not so much from its own intrinsic nature as from its first application to human uses —that is, from the Dance—and assume only such plastic forms as spring naturally and freely from the nature of the dramatic subject it seeks to illustrate. The second point is what is known as the *Leitmotiv*.

Be it said at once that the *Leitmotiv* idea— the association of a theme, or musical phrase, with a particular personage, idea, or incident in a drama—was not original with Wagner; neither do we find anything new in his use of it until we come to his third manner.*

---

* Manifold attempts have proved the hopelessness of trying to discover the first appearance of the *Leitmotiv* in dramatic music. Let only two pre-Wagnerian instances of it be mentioned here.

In Mozart's *Don Giovanni*, the duel between the Don and the Commendatore is accompanied in the orchestra by a series of

The episodic use of the *Leitmotiv* was no new thing; and all that distinguishes Wagner's use of it in his earlier operas — from *Rienzi* to *Lohengrin*—is that it is more frequent than is to be found in other composers. But, in the last struggle between Tannhäuser and Wolfram (in the third act of *Tannhäuser*), still more, in the scene on the church steps between Ortrud and Telramund (in the second act of *Lohengrin*), we begin to find something of the use Wagner makes of the *Leitmotiv* in his later music-dramas. This use is no longer merely episodic, but distinctly functional. In Wagner's third manner, almost the whole web of the music is woven out of *Leitmotiven ;* they come either

---

rapid ascending scales, alternately in the first violins and the basses; these scales suggest the quickly-alternating sword-thrusts. In the closing scene of the opera, when the statue of the dead Commendatore has got the libertine hero by the hand, and is urging him to repent, these same scales return in the orchestra—but now only in the basses, the violins (Don Giovanni's sword) being silenced, showing this second, ideal struggle between the two combatants to be merely one-sided.

Again, in Meyerbeer's *Robert le Diable*, when Alice, Robert's foster-sister, calls his attention to the likeness between his friend Bertram and the Fiend's face in the picture of St. Michael and the Dragon in the old church in her native village, the orchestra takes up the theme of Raimbaut's ballad, " *Jadis régnait en Normandie*," in which the young pilgrim had previously told the story of Robert's birth and infernal parentage. The listener sees at once that Bertram is the Evil One in person, and Robert's father.

singly and in succession, or else simultaneously and interwoven.* There is no melodic constituent of the music that is not a *Leitmotiv*. This gives the music, if not greater dramatic force, at least an unflagging dramatic suggestiveness.

Such was Wagner's theory in its main outlines ; of details like alliterative verse, infinite melody, and *das Reinmenschliche* in general, nothing need be said here.† This theory he applied fully in all the works of his third period — the *Nibelungen* tetralogy, *Tristan und Isolde, Die Meistersinger von Nürnberg*, and *Par-*

---

* A particularly complex example is the closing *stretto* in C major of the great love-scene between Siegfried and Brünnhilde, in the third act of *Siegfried*. Here the music is woven out of five distinct *Leitmotiven*.

† The elaborate treatise on the *Stabreim* (alliterative rhyme) in *Oper und Drama* is but another proof of how much more Wagner had the artistic than the philosophico-critical temperament, in his readiness to elevate any passing fad into an eternal truth. He was already at work on the text of *Der Ring des Nibelungen ;* and the appropriateness of the old Teutonic *Stabreim* to the poetic treatment of a subject taken from the folk-lore of the race would naturally not escape him. But he used the *Stabreim* only in the *Ring ;* his other texts (on Romance subjects) are in ordinary rhymed verse, occasionally in blank verse.

As for "*das Reinmenschliche* (the Purely Human)" about which he talks so much, one may agree with Immanuel Flohjäger that, in Wagner's conception, it differed little, in the last analysis, from Don Giovanni's "*sostegno e gloria d'umanità.*" (*Don Giovanni*, Act II., scene 14.)

sifal; the practical artistic expression of it was his third manner.

And now, apart from all considerations of theory, also apart from all questions of individual style, exactly what was the fundamental principle of this third manner of Wagner's, as a musico-dramatic method? Considered from this point of view, we find the third manner to be little else than a higher development of something quite old, of a method largely employed by the Italians of the first half of the nineteenth century, and traceable back at least as far as Mozart—if not considerably farther.

Both Mozart and the Italians who came after him often wrote passages in which the musical development was carried on entirely by the orchestra, while the text was delivered by the singers in a style which ran (according to the nature of the sentiments to be expressed) all the way from the bald rhetorical colloquialism of the *recitativo secco* to the more dramatic stress of " grand " recitative, and even to the poignant expressiveness of distinctly melodic phrases. Considered from a purely musical point of view, the only connection between the voice-parts and the orchestra was that the two went well together; but what the orchestra played was a self-consistent musical development, not in any true sense an accompaniment; the voice-parts oscillated between the purely rhetorical and the musically significant. The prototype of the Wagnerian method is to be found in the first part (*Allegro*) of Leporello's " *Madamina, il catalogo è questo*," and Don Giovanni's "*Metà di voi quà vadano.*" * Of course, the musical style is very different indeed; but the musico-dramatic method is essentially the same. The whole business is but a higher musical development of the old *recitativo stromentato ;* a higher dramatic development was hardly possible.

If Wagner's third manner is found fully developed in *Das Rheingold* (the first of the *Ring* dramas, written in 1853–54), we do not find his style completely matured and individualized, nor his technique fully grown, until we come to *Siegfried* (the third drama of the *Ring* tetralogy, begun in 1857).† Completely Wagnerian

---

* Other examples of this sort of thing are: nearly the whole of the first part of the finale (No. 9) to the second act of Donizetti's *Lucia di Lammermoor* (up to the beginning of the sestettino, "*Chi mi frena ?* "); the first few pages of the final quartet (No. 23) in Verdi's *Il trovatore* (up to Leonora's " *Prima che d'altrui vivere*"). Such passages are common enough with composers of that school.

† It has generally been deemed convenient to date the full development of Wagner's musical individuality and technique with *Tristan* (begun in 1857, after stopping short half-way through the second act of *Siegfried*); but the full development of style and individuality stares one in the face from the very first page of

though the method may be, there is not a little in *Das Rheingold* and *Die Walküre* that is not wholly Wagner's; not only are some of the themes appropriated from other composers, having not quite the true later-Wagner ring, but even up to far on in *Die Walküre* does one find now and then a distinctly Meyerbeerish detail.* Wagner, like other great men, had a way of taking his own where he found it; but, with *Siegfried*, he began to find it only in himself.

Siegfried. Not the faintest difference in style is to be detected between the first and second halves of Act II. (the second half was not begun till 1865; that is after the whole of *Tristan und Isolde* and most of the *Meistersinger* had been written); whereas a marked difference in style is to be noted between the third act of *Die Walküre* and the first of *Siegfried*.

As a matter of mere technique, compare the whole musical development of the scene between Brünnhilde and Siegmund (*Die Walküre*, Act II., sc. 4) with that of the very similar scene between The Wanderer and Mime (*Siegfried*, Act I, sc. 2), and see how vastly more secure is the technical skill shown in the latter.

* One of the Rhine-daughter themes is taken from Mendelssohn's *Schöne Melusine* ; the theme beginning at Siemund's "*Der dir nun folgt, wohin führst du den Helden?*" (*Walküre*, Act II., sc. 4) comes from Marschner's *Der Vampyr*. The sobbing figure in the 'celli under Brünnhilde's "*War es so ehrlos, was ich beging, dass mein Vergeh'n nun die Ehre mir raubt?*" (*Walküre*, Act III., sc. 3) is nothing if not very familiar and characteristic Meyerbeer. Wagner owed much to Meyerbeer from the first, and only succeeded in ridding himself entirely of his influence with the beginning of *Siegfried*.

Not the least merit of Wagner's third manner is its wondrous flexibility and adaptability.
It can lend itself to every conceivable kind of
drama, from the most exalted tragedy to the
broadest farce. In its more colloquial phase it
becomes the first German substitute for the
Italian *recitativo quasi-parlando* ever discovered,
a fit musical vehicle for homely dialogue. Nor
does it lose caste amid the grandest and most
elaborate musical developments. It is at once
thoroughly dramatic and thoroughly musical.

The general consensus of the world seems
to be to-day that Wagner's greatest works are
Tristan und Isolde, the infinite tragedy (brought
out in Munich in 1865), and *Die Meistersinger von
Nürnberg*, the homely comedy (originally con-
ceived as a satirical counterpart to *Tannhäuser*,
brought out in Munich in 1868). These two
are probably the only works for the lyric stage
which, for poetry and intellectuality of conception, perfection of execution, vividness of character-drawing, and general wealth of genius at
its highest, can justly be ranked with Mozart's
Don Giovanni. Of the two, *Tristan* may be
deemed the more temporal and evanescent, it
sums up the whole nineteenth century, the
whole "Now" of artistic feeling ; *Die Meistersinger* has more of the monumental, of the eternally valid.

If it is difficult to determine which was the dominant bent of Wagner's genius,—the musical, the dramatic, or the poetico-picturesque,— one can hardly escape recognizing the dominant trait of his character to have been combative energy. He was a born fighter; with his well-nigh excessive craving for human sympathy, his character was distinctly militant. Adverse criticism hurt him sorely; it seemed to him a wanton refusal of that sympathy which, his whole nature told him, he had a right to demand of the world. But it spurred him on, was the stimulant which his militant genius most needed. Indeed, one can hardly help suspecting that the opposition he met with during the better part of his life may have been for something in shaping his work, and that much therein might have been different without it.* He was not in the least an intellectual hermit, could not live happily out of communion with the rest of mankind. Not that his thirst for sympathy ever led him to alter his course by an iota for the sake of winning it,— there was not a grain of diplomacy in his composition, and he carried firmness to the pitch of obstinacy,—but that, he looking instinctively upon sympathy as his natural right, it set his

---

* In this respect, Wagner was very like another militant genius, who, in most others, is his diametrical opposite: Émile Zola.

moral teeth on edge to find that, where he had asked for bread, he was offered a stone. He found the whole world out of joint, and was fully persuaded that he was the predestined man to set it right. Opposition was but fuel to his energy. With every successive work he brought forth, he seemed to say to the world: You found that, in my last work, I had gone too far in my chosen direction; well, here you will see that I have gone still farther!*

Probably the finest practical illustration of Wagner's indomitable energy and faith in himself was his conception and carrying-out of the Bayreuth scheme. This was to be the setting

---

* Nothing could have shown more characteristically Wagner's craving for sympathy, his inflexibility in face of opposition, and also a certain naïve inability of his to look at things otherwise than from his own point of view, than his writing *Tristan und Isolde* in 1857. He was half-way through the score of his *Nibelungen-Ring*, and interrupted his work because he felt an imperative need of renewing his relations with the general public, which had been severed ever since *Lohengrin ;* and the completion, let alone the production, of the *Ring* seemed then in a very dim and distant future. He accordingly set to work upon something which he thought would easily renew his relations with the public at large, something "simple and easily brought-out," not even requiring the paraphernalia of a court opera-house. And this work was *Tristan*, which was given up in despair, as "impossible," after nearly sixty rehearsals at the Vienna Hofoper, and, when at last produced in Munich, called forth a shriek of utter dismay from all but a few determined adherents. It was probably the direst disappointment of his life.

right of a disjointed world, as thorough a destruction and reorganization of social operatic conditions as his Music-Drama itself was of the artistic form of the Opera — an event quite unique in the history of that form of art! *
Seemingly wild as this Bayreuth scheme was, Wagner's energy made it a success—at least, in so far as he actually brought the Festspielhaus and the performances into being. Wellnigh everything at Bayreuth was new: a new form of Lyric Drama was there to be given under new conditions; it was to be the death-knell, not only of the old Opera, but of the old Opera-House as well.

In speaking of Bayreuth, one enters upon delicate, quasi-political ground. The institution already has a history, but does not quite belong to history; it is still active. Yet Bayreuth has been so important a factor in the artistic life of the world for hard upon a quarter of a century, that it is impossible not to try to sum up the main results of the experiment— so far.

---

* Unique, yes—as a whole. But how old some details are! Remember how, at Bayreuth, the beginning of every act is announced by apposite *Leitmotiven*, played on brass instruments. Well, at the performance of Monteverdi's *Orfeo*, in Mantua in 1607, the signals for raising the curtain were every time given by trumpets.

Like the only other institution in the world which at all resembles it (if with some important differences), the Comédie - Française in Paris, Bayreuth has helped teach one valuable lesson : that the first principle of all dramatic performance whatsoever is infinite painstaking and sinking the individual in the coöperative mass. To this principle Bayreuth has been unswervingly true from the first; this, too, has been the prime element in what artistic success it has had.

As a repository for firmly-established, authentic, and authoritative traditions, on the other hand, Bayreuth has been considerably a failure. Yet such a repository Wagner intended it primarily to be ; this was perhaps the part of his dream he had most at heart. That he, of all men, should have thought such a dream realizable seems strange ; for, of all men, he best knew how traditions are formed, and how they are (not) perpetuated. But the thing seemed to him so indispensable that he could not but believe it possible.

If anything in this world is perishable, liable above all else to deterioration and falsification, that thing is what is called a " tradition of performance." No true artist feels himself legitimately bound by it ; and, in this matter, true and sham artists unfortunately agree. A work of art may be what we call "eternal," good for a very considerable time; but a style of performance, no matter how authentic, is in its very nature transitory; the world, sooner or later, outgrows its validity. A style of performance which is really admirable always reflects something of the spirit of its own time; in this way only can it be fully intelligible, comprehensible. And it may truly be said that the surest test of a work of art's having some of the eternal essence in it is its power of adapting itself, in its voyage down the centuries, to successive, ever-changing styles of performance. If a work of art reflect, or embody, nothing more than the special spirit of its own time, then is its span of life measured; for it is only by being ever fresh and new that it can hope to live. And, if it does so keep itself new, the new style will fit it as well as the old; nay, better, for it will be the most faithful mirror of its newness. Not anchylosed tradition, but keen, profound, vital understanding is the surest guide to the correct performance of such works as Wagner's music-dramas. And, if authentic traditions are no sure guide, what shall be said of unauthentic, or falsified ones?

In so far as regards the establishment of authentic traditions, Bayreuth may well be said to have been a failure from the beginning.

Only through Wagner's succeeding in completely realizing his ideal could it have been in any degree a success. And, even in the performances given in his own lifetime at Bayreuth, Wagner really fell considerably short of his ideal.* With a few distinguished exceptions, he was absolutely unable to get the executive forces he needed; they did not exist! All he could do was the best he could. The result was that the *Ring* performances in 1876, and those of *Parsifal* in 1882, were by no means impeccable models; together with much that was admirable, there were many serious blemishes. And, as years went by, some of the worst blemishes were allowed to crystallize into "traditions," while much that was authentically good was more and more forgotten.†

---

* Remember that sharply-criticised item in his speech at the congratulatory banquet: "So far have we brought it; it now remains for you to complete the work, then we *shall have* a German Art!"

† Lapses even from the standard of 1876 and 1882 crept in almost immediately. As early as 1884 (under Scaria's stage-management, too!) the author saw with his own eyes Winkelmann-Parsifal do a thing on the stage fit to make Wagner turn in his grave. After Gurnemanz's first rebuke for killing the swan, Mr. Winkelmann coolly nodded to someone behind the scenes, and then, without the faintest attempt at concealment, tossed his bow off the stage, to be caught in the wings. *Der Unglückliche!*—as Mr. Carl Armbruster exclaimed, on hearing the story.

In a word, Bayreuth fell, little by little, into incompetent hands.

The principle of starting where the original authority (the composer) left off, and then proceeding thence in your own way, according to the dictates of your own artistic sense, is excellent in itself; upon the whole, the only sound principle. But, as Captain Bunsby would say, the virtue of it lies in its application. When applied by highly cultivated, that is, competent, professional musicians, it is one thing; when applied by strenuous amateurs, no matter how sincere or gifted, it is quite another. And the trouble at Bayreuth has been that the management of the performances there has fallen more and more into the hands of amateurs; the thoroughly competent musicians, who knew what they were about, have been more and more compelled to quit the field in disgust—to save their own artistic dignity. The practical upshot of all of which is that the only reason of being to which Bayreuth can still lay just claim is that infinite pains-taking, which has never once been intermitted. If Bayreuth has gone wrong, it has gone carefully and most laboriously wrong. But only in this one matter of pains-taking can it still stand before the world as a model.

To take up but one instance of the formation

and perpetuation of a bad tradition, it is worth noting that the very worst defects of German singing have been actually raised to the dignity of an authoritative "school" at Bayreuth. The world is told, and in no faltering voice, that a style of singing which Wagner abhorred, against which he protested, detail by detail, in his writings, with all the force of his indignant and scornful dialectics, and the direct opposite of which he advocated—the world is told that this style is the authentic standard norm for Wagnerian singing.*

Upon the whole, Bayreuth is no longer a trustworthy guide. If the world is henceforth to look anywhere for guidance in the matter of performing Wagner's music-dramas, it must look where it always has looked in similar cases: to competent, educated, and experienced professional musicians, even though they wear no "official" badge of authority; the strenuous amateur can have no word to say. If the Bay-

---

* One strongly suspects the advocates of this abominable style of making a virtue out of necessity. When we hear, for instance, a man like Mr. Ernest van Dyck openly proclaim it to be authentically Wagnerian, we are reminded of what the late Robert Franz once wrote of Dr. Philipp Spitta's "Defense" of his harshly-criticised accompaniments to Frederick the Great's flute works: "The whole scribble is an *oratio pro domo*, delivered by a thoroughly incompetent man upon himself!" *Vide* also on this head Mr. W. J. HENDERSON, in *The Score* for September, 1900.

reuth idea is ever worthily to be incarnated,— and there can be no doubt that the idea was very dear to Wagner,—it can be so incarnated only through the efforts of practical musicians, who know what is artistic and what absurd. Will it ever be wholly incarnated? Probably not; at least, not until all our old social operatic conditions shall have been destroyed and reorganized, and a disjointed world set right in Wagner's way—and then Bayreuth's occupation will be gone, for the incarnation will be universal.

The world accepts an artist's work, not on his terms, but on its own. And, if the conditions under which it accepts it are inadequate or antagonistic, they can be changed for the better only by the work itself; by a better and completer understanding of it forcing the appreciation and conviction of their inadequacy and antagonism upon the world at large, and its rising to the emergency, and curing them.

IX

The Development of the Art of the Opera-Singer

THE opera-singer is at once a singer and an actor; herein lies the difficulty of his artistic problem. The difficulty, but hardly the peculiarity; for, as, ever since the establishment of the Opera, nearly all the greatest singers of the world have been opera-singers,—that is, artists whose task of singing was more or less complicated by the task of histrionic action,—the influence which their example has exerted upon the Art of Singing in general has been to a greater or less extent affected (if only mediately, or by ricochet) by the histrionic side of their professional work. By this no more is meant than that the great opera-singers, being both in the majority and in a more prominent position before the public than the merely concert-singing minority, have at all times set the standard of artistic singing; and, in so far as their own singing was affected by the fact of their acting, the standard they set must have been to some extent affected by it, too.

As the Art of Singing, as we now know it, has been developed mainly on the operatic stage, one can see that its development must necessarily have gone forward under conditions many of which were unfavourable, even antagonistic. Conditions which render the perfect exercise of any art more difficult than it is in its own nature are nothing if not unfavourable; and, to the Art of Singing, histrionic action is one of these. The easiest situation for the singer is one in which he has to think of nothing but his singing, in which he has to make no physical nor mental effort beside that of singing. The bodily exercise of acting, the mental exercise of having to deal with musical difficulties,—complexities of structure, rhythmic anomalies, or hazardous intonations,—even the mere fact of having to specialize his expression of the poetic text, all these place difficulties in the singer's path. And the opera-singer has always had, in greater or less degree, to face and conquer one or more of these. It may even be said that, ever since the first period of great singing of which we have any definite knowledge, these difficulties in the singer's path have been pretty steadily on the increase.

Taking the arts of singing and of acting separately, and looking at them from the psychical point of view, we find that the general course

of development which the Art of Singing has
pursued has been, either steadily or intermit-
tently, from the comparatively mechanical toward the more expressive, from the apathetic
toward the emotional; that the general course
pursued by the Art of Acting has been from
the conventional toward the realistic, from the
more or less vivid exposition of character toward the real-seeming impersonation of character—that is, from mere impressiveness toward
verisimilitude. And both these propositions
hold good with the gradual development of
that combination of the two arts which is the
opera-singer's business. It will be well to bear
this in mind.

Of what the Art of Singing was before 1700
we have no exact knowledge; we know, to be
sure, that there was the Archilei in 1595 with
her "*giri e gruppi*," and can surmise that she
was neither the first nor the only one of her
kind; but of how she sang her flourishes we
know nothing at all. The earliest source to
which the *bel canto*—as we now know it from
singers like Marcella Sembrich, Nellie Melba,
Jean de Reszke, and (alas!) too few others—has
been authentically traced is the singing-school
founded at Bologna, about 1700, by Francesco
Antonio Pistocchi (1659–?). He and his pupil
Antonio Bernacchi (1690–1756) have commonly

been regarded as the Fathers of Italian singing. They probably were not quite that; but, in lack of earlier documents, one must risk the "make-believe of a beginning" somewhere. At all events, it is safe to assume that the Art of Singing pure and simple, in its most highly perfected form, what we know as the *Arte del bel canto*, originated in Italy. It has been cultivated all over the musical world; but, wherever it has been cultivated well, it has been cultivated on Italian principles. With a regard for truth rather than for the *amour propre* of other nations, we can take the best Italian singing as the standard norm.

So it will be well to begin our study of the history of the opera-singer's art with a critical examination of Italian examples. Italian singing has had two great culminating periods, two zeniths, each of which was illustrated by a group of great singers; let us, for the nonce, confine our examination to these.*

---

* Of course, to believe contemporary accounts, there never was a time when the Art of Singing was not going headlong to the dogs; neither, to believe the same accounts, was there ever a time when some few supreme artists had not brought it to a higher pitch of perfection than it had ever reached before, or would ever realize again—thus making the favoured listener's grandparents and grandchildren equally worthy objects for pity. But, between these two contradictory extremes, patient History must pursue her sane middle course.

The first group is made up of pupils of Pistocchi, Bernacchi, and other contemporary teachers.* Note, as significant, that it belongs to the Handel, or " Oratorio" period of Opera, to the period when the Opera had drifted farthest away from the Drama, when its music was least dramatic and scenic, and admitted of the least accompanying histrionic action; that is, to the period when conditions were most favourable to pure singing.

There is no reason for doubting that these great singers of the Handel period brought the *bel canto* to as high a pitch of perfection as has ever been known, that, in matters of artistic melodic phrasing and vocal technique (including production of tone, command of breath, pure intonation, and smooth agility of vocalization) they have hardly, perhaps never, been surpassed. But remember the conditions under which they sang. " In the days of the Schools of the *Arte del bel canto*, the masters did not have to take truth of expression (*l'expression juste*) into account, for the singer was not required to render the sentiments of the *dramatis personæ* with verisimilitude; all that was

---

* Nicolini (1673- ?), Senesino (1680- ?), Francesca Cuzzoni (1700–1770), Faustina Hasse (1700–1783), Caffarelli (1703–1783), Farinelli (1705–1782), Carestini (1705- ?), Gizziello (1714–1761), Pacchiarotti (1744- ?), and others.

demanded of him was harmonious sounds, the *bel canto*." * In other words, beauty of vocal tone and beauty of musical plastics were the only recognized elements of emotional expression in singing, beyond that general fervour of delivery which may best be described as an absence of apathy; the emotions themselves were not to be differentiated, the psychical character of the *dramatis persona* was not to be taken into account, all the singer had to do was to sing—and nothing else.† And, to interfere with the perfection of his singing, he had little or no acting to do; at most, a conventional oratorical gesture or two, such as it would often be more of an effort for an Italian to omit than to perform. The only item to interfere with the singer's devoting his whole attention to his production of tone, melodic phrasing, and *coloratura* was a certain undeniable complexity in the structure of the music he sang; such airs

---

* VICTOR MAUREL, *Dix ans de carrière*, 171. Paris: Paul Dupont, 1897.

† Let this not seem improbable to the sentimentally disposed. A noteworthy example of this sort of thing is still fresh in the memory of the present older generation: Pasquale Brignoli. This admirable singer never even tried to throw emotion into his singing, any more than he tried to act; yet he would often arouse audiences to the frenetic pitch of excitement, and coolly draw tears from many an eye—by sheer beauty of tone and perfection of musical plastics.

as Handel's do not quite sing themselves, they often contain purely musical difficulties, especially in the relation of the voice-part to the accompaniment, such as only a trained musician can master with ease. And the great singers of this period were, as a rule, good enough musicians to prevent such musical difficulties being an obstacle to the excellence of their singing.

The second culminating period of Italian singing coincides with the Rossini-Donizetti-Bellini period of Opera in its hey-day, and is best represented by the group of artists who sang at the Théâtre-Italien (salle Ventadour) in Paris in the 'thirties and 'forties of the nineteenth century.*

Here we find the conditions considerably altered. The music is at once more dramatic and more scenic; it gives larger opportunity for differentiating and specializing the emotions, larger scope for histrionic action. The

---

* Luigi Lablache (1794–1858), Giovanni Battista Rubini (1795–1854), Antonio Tamburini (1800–1876), Maria Felicità Malibran (born Garcia, 1808–1836), Giuseppe Mario (1810–1883), Giorgio Ronconi (1810–1890), Giulia Grisi (1811–1869), Fanny Persiani (1812–1867), and Marietta Alboni (1823–still living). Alboni came a little late into the group, in 1847; Malibran was the first to die out of it, in 1836, and Rubini retired in 1843. As another surpassingly fine representative of the style may be mentioned Jenny Lind (1820–1887).

old alternation between *secco* recitative and set aria has been much modified, and the dramatic *scena* invented. The singing must still be the *bel canto*, but great intensity of dramatic stress of accent is demanded ; furthermore, Rubini has introduced the *vibrato*, the full stress of vocal energy that stops just short of being a *tremolo*, or "wobble." The opera-singer of this period has more to do than his predecessor of Handel's time : he must sing not only well but dramatically, he must do at least something in the way of histrionic action. Yet there is no reason for doubting that this great group of singers sang fully as well, in all matters of vocal technique and melodic phrasing, as the Handelians did.

How is this to be accounted for? Principally by the well-nigh child-like simplicity of the music, and the enormous skill with which the composers of the period adapted it to the human voice. In Handel's day, the musical structure was essentially contrapuntal, that is, an harmonious interweaving of several interdependent parts (or "voices"), of which the voice-part was, like the Pope among the bishops, but "*primus inter pares.*" In singing music of this sort, the singer has to mind his P's and Q's, to bear constantly in mind that what he sings is no independent entity in itself, but only one strand in a complex fabric; for the performance not to come to grief (especially in the absence of an orchestral conductor), such music must be sung strictly in time; only in free cadenzas and closing cadences can the singer venture safely upon modifications of the rhythm. But, under Rossini, Donizetti, and Bellini, the voice-part had become entirely liberated from its contrapuntal interconnection with the orchestral parts. The voice-part was absolutely and unreservedly "*primus*," and there were no "*pares*" left; the orchestral parts had resolved themselves into a subordinate accompaniment, the chief object of which was to support and buoy up the singer. Moreover, the orchestral conductor had come into existence, and his business was to see to it that the accompaniment followed the singer, who was accordingly quite free to take his own time, commit what rhythmic indiscretions he found convenient, and so make things easy for himself. The general structure of Rossini's, Donizetti's, and Bellini's music is clarity itself, a clarity "clearer than crystal"; were it not for the *coloratura*, a child might sing it. And, though this *coloratura* can be mastered by nothing short of an enormous vocal technique, it is in one important respect intrinsically easier than Handel's, inasmuch as the vocal

" effects" are purely and simply *vocal* effects, written with sole regard for graceful and elegant performance by the human voice, and not in the least influenced by structural considerations. The Rossini-Donizetti-Bellini *coloratura* is, for the most part, purely ornamental, a sort of efflorescence of the melody; it plays no real part in the musical development, is not thematic, as Handel's is.

It is important to recognize that, in this period, although the demand for emotional expression, intensity of dramatic accent, and at least something of histrionism, made the singer's task harder and more complicated than it had been before, these untoward conditions were more than compensated for by entirely favourable musical ones. So the opera-singer's vocal art suffered no real prejudice.

A comparison of these two great periods of Italian singing indicates the direction matters have taken with the opera-singer from Handel's time down to our own. From then to now, he has had to face an ever-increasing accumulation of untoward conditions; his professional work has become more and more complicated. From Rossini's time down to this, the purely musical difficulties he has had to face have been constantly on the increase—complexity of musical structure, rhythmic complications, hazardous intonations; he has had to fight against a more and more brilliant style of instrumentation, often pushed to a point where the greatest stress of vocal effort is required of him, to make himself heard above the orchestral din; more and better acting is demanded of him, he finds the vague generalities of histrionism no longer of avail, for these must make way for a highly specialized, real-seeming dramatic impersonation; intellectually and physically his task has been doubled and trebled. Above all, the sheer nervous tension of situations and music has so increased as to make due self-control on his part less and less easy.* The opera-singer's position to-day is verily no joke; he has to face and conquer difficulties such as the great *bel-cantists* of the Handel period never dreamt of. And, to equip himself for holding his own, as a singer, amid all these antagonistic conditions, it must be admitted that he has, for the most part, taken little pains.

If ever there were human mortal who, for the last fifty years or so, had steadfastly refused

---

* The late Max Alvary once said that, considering the emotional intensity of music and situations, the constant coöperation of the surging orchestra, and, most of all, the unconquerable feeling of the reality of it all, it was a wonder that singing actors did not go stark mad, before the very faces of the audience, in parts like Tristan or Siegfried.

to look his peculiar situation squarely in the face, and size it up wisely for his own artistic good, that mortal is the average opera-singer. The one fact that florid *coloratura* has been steadily on the decline in vocal writing, and is now virtually obsolete, has led foolish singers to believe that the old perfection of vocal technique is no longer indispensable; and they have acted accordingly. A generation after Rossini and his Italian contemporaries had begun running away from conservatories before their musical education was half finished, budding Italian singers began to imitate them; the same has been, to a great extent, true in France also. And, as for the Germans, they have, for the most part, but added stronger and stronger emphasis to their inborn and carefully nurtured contempt for vocal technique in all its phases. Here is a spectacle for the world to gape at: the spectacle of a race of born and bred musicians, intellectually, emotionally, and poetically gifted, on the average, far beyond their colleagues in other countries, filled with the profoundest love and respect for their art, yet fondly expecting to do the greatest things in dramatic singing without even the rudiments of a special technique — that is, absolutely without the power of doing! No doubt there have been, and still are, great German singers, especially women; but, when really great, they have sung in the Italian, not in the German, way.

The solemn truth—and too few appreciate how solemn—is that the opera-singer to-day needs ten-fold the vocal technique that he ever needed before. The banishment of *coloratura* is but one jot in his favour, all the other conditions are cumulatively against him; moreover, their antagonism to pure singing is augmenting in an ever-increasing ratio. The old times when a singer, who did not know a note of music and could not count four to the measure to save his life, could yet "sing like a god" are gone, never to return. The singer of to-day must be a musician to boot, or he has a sorry chance of doing great work; but he must also, and even primarily, be a *singer*—which last too many are prone to forget.

X

The Present

SINCE Wagner's death, in 1883, the most interesting fact in the history of the Opera
has been the gradual spread of his influence.
And, in this connection, it may be well to spe-
cify at once exactly what is meant by Wagner's
influence.

Wagner's style, or manner, has, upon the
whole, been little imitated. Some composers,
even among those of note, have at times written themes which, without actual plagiarism,
more or less resemble certain *Leitmotive* in his
music-dramas;* yet no more than some of Wagner's own recall those of other composers. But
Wagner's themes are, after all, not always so
inveterately individual as his general style—
his harmony, modes of development, and musi-

---

* Some themes in Anton Bruckner's fifth symphony, in E major,
for instance, so strongly recall Wagner that a certain musician
once exclaimed, on hearing the symphony, that it sounded "as if
the composer had been to Bayreuth in too dazed a mental condition to remember the themes aright."

cal structure; and this style of his is so absolutely his own that it could hardly be success-
fully imitated, save in the way of parody. If
by Wagner's influence is meant the influence of
his musical individuality, it may fairly be said
to have been null. In this respect, Wagner
has had no more followers than Mozart or
Beethoven; he has founded no "school." *

But, on the other hand, the influence of
Wagner's ideas concerning the Lyric Drama,
as a form of art, has been very potent and far-
reaching indeed; and none the less so for being
seldom responded to *en bloc*. Hardly a com
poser has reflected the influence of all Wagner's principles at once; some of them seem to
have appealed to one, others to another. The
too commonly applied test — the more or less
extensive use of the *Leitmotiv* — is fallacious;
for hardly a single composer since Wagner has
used the *Leitmotiv* quite in his way: as the sole
thematic material out of which the musical
fabric is woven. And, as has been pointed out
in Chapter VIII., the merely episodic use of the
Leitmotiv, no matter how frequent, is not essentially Wagnerian. In fine, what is here meant

---

* Of the few quasi-imitators Wagner has had may well be said,
as Mendelssohn said of the handful of men who tried to write *à la*
Beethoven in his time: "They clear their throats as he did, and
cough his cough; but that is as far as they get!"

by the spread of Wagner's influence is the immense effect the prime gist of his doctrines has had upon opera-writing in general since the publication of *Das Kunstwerk der Zukunft* and *Oper und Drama*, and, most especially, since his operas and music-dramas have come to be performed outside of Germany. This prime gist is the abandoning of such musical forms as are not directly determined by the text and dramatic action, and the recognition of text and action as the sole musical form-determining principles in the Lyric Drama. Though few composers have gone to such lengths in the practical application of this principle as Wagner, the tendency to apply it less and less partially has been strongly marked well-nigh everywhere.

Beside this fact of the spread of the Wagner influence, two others now claim our attention: the operatic premiership of Giuseppe Verdi, and the recent musical renascence in Italy. All three are curiously interconnected.

As the musical decadence in Italy, which set in shortly after Cimarosa,* was the result of over-exportation, with no importation to counterbalance it, and of a consequent course of musical in-breeding, no musical renascence could have come about without a cessation of

---

* *Vide* Chapter V., pages 93–96.

these conditions. That the nation should go on forever as it had been going for well over half a century was impossible; that way ruin lay. That its eyes would, sooner or later, be opened to the folly of its course was highly probable. And Italy did at last awaken to a consciousness of the baneful effects of her long attempt to live wholly on her own musical resources, almost to their total exhaustion. About the middle 'sixties, Italy began to come to a realizing sense of having fallen behind in the race for musical glory. A keen-eyed Chesterfield might have detected premonitory symptoms of an impending revolution; the musical atmosphere was plainly growing electric, and any more than usually violent disturbance might produce the spark, and with it a momentous shock.

The disturbance came in the shape of the performance, under Angelo Mariani, of Wagner's *Lohengrin* in Bologna in 1868. Young musical Italy (or North Italy) felt the shock, and put on its thinking-cap. The revolution came, its focus being Milan. As with other revolutions, its first practical expression was negative and destructive; its next, positive and constructive. Naturally enough, the first bolt of protest struck Verdi; from being the acknowledged crowned head and demigod, he suddenly— possibly to his surprise, but certainly not at all

to his dismay—found himself hooted at as the
crying shame of Italian Music—as the "hand-
organ man!" But a positive, constructive
movement was at hand.

"Verdi's gleaming star seemed near extinction, about the early 'seventies. At least, so
said the young Milanese Hotspurs. To be
sure, his last two operas, *La forza del destino*
and *Don Carlos*, first produced abroad and afterwards more or less adversely criticised in Italy,
had been followed by a third, which brought
Verdi's genius fully to light again; still, the
popularity of *Aïda* was really not much believed in in Italy. Verdi had written it for
the then Khédive, Ismaïl Pasha, for the opening of the Suez Canal and the accompanying
festivities, and had won an enormous success
with it in Cairo. But Milanese musical youth
—*i progressisti*—agreed, all the same, that the
Busseto master was completely written out, and
that it was high time for 'another and a wor-
thier' to come and mount the musical throne of
Italy. The first waves of Wagnerian enthusiasm were beginning to swell; a threatening
storm—threatening the fragile edifices of modern Italian Music — was blowing across the
Alps, and premonitory revolutionary symptoms
were diagnostically observable. A mutinous,
hot-blooded element, made up mostly of Conser-

vatory pupils in their 'storm-and-stress period,' with the advantage of a solid musical education, summoned up all its subtlety to prove to the astonished older generation that it had hitherto been the victim of a degenerate musical Baal-worship, and that all music from Rossini down to his last follower, Verdi, had nothing in common with the true, uncounterfeited Art of Tones; that the true Evangel was now, for the first time, preached in the timid attempts to introduce Wagner's operas, and that everyone's eyes would be opened!

" Bach, Beethoven, and Schumann, who had hitherto been known only by name in Italy, especially as regards their larger works, then formed the firm classical foundation of Milanese musical youth, thanks to an enlightened body of teachers; and they thought that, armed with these weapons, they might fearlessly give battle to the bear-baiting Philistines. If you observed the long-haired Conservatory folk in the streets, you could see that the times were mightily changed, and that, instead of pianoforte-scores of the 'ever-young' *Sonnambula*, *Norma*, *Lucia*, *Lucrezia*, *Trovatore*, and *Traviata*, they now carried fat volumes of Bach's B minor Mass, *Don Giovanni*, *The Seasons*, *Freischütz*, Schubert's and Schumann's symphonies, *Lohengrin*, and *Tannhäuser* under their arms. Even

Mendelssohn and Spohr were an '*überwundener Standpunkt*' in their eyes." *

But, when *Aïda* came to be better known in Italy, and the Manzoni *Requiem* was brought out (in 1874), the "young Hotspurs" found that Verdi had really been beforehand with them; that the new formula, which he had but stammered in *La forza* and *Don Carlos*, was here uttered with unmistakable distinctness, and that Verdi was surprisingly abreast of the times; nay more, that a patient study of Sebastian Bach † had given him a technique such as need not blush to face any judge in Europe. Verdi was reinstated on the Italian musical throne, and, having now doffed his hand-organ manhood, led the revolution.

When *Otello* was produced in 1887, it showed that *Aïda* had been by no means Verdi's last word in Opera, and that, notwithstanding the fact that Wagner's *Tristan*, *Meistersinger*, and *Nibelungen-Ring* had come up in the interim, old Verdi was still well up with the age. ‡ And,

---

* Abridged from MARTIN ROEDER, in the *Program-Books* of the Boston Symphony Orchestra, 1894–95, pages 54–57.

† Open volumes of Bach's works had long covered the pianoforte and all available table-room in Verdi's study.

‡ *Tristan und Isolde* and *Die Meistersinger von Nürnberg* were, to be sure, brought out in Munich in 1865 and 1868 respectively. But neither made much headway in the world, especially outside

if *Otello* failed to convince everyone of this, *Falstaff* (brought out in 1893) carried full conviction with it.

In *Otello*, and especially in *Falstaff*, Verdi spoke the newest word yet spoken in Italian Opera; *Falstaff* is still miles ahead of his later followers. Much has been said both affirming and denying the influence of Wagner; and it may be admitted at once that the two men's styles are utterly different. Verdi is as thoroughly Italian as Wagner is German; but this is not the point. In *Falstaff* we find the plastic form of the music conditioned by nothing but the text and the dramatic action; and, no matter what this form may be, this one fact is, of itself, enough to stamp the formula of *Falstaff* as essentially Wagnerian. Moreover, Verdi has gone to greater lengths in his application of this Wagnerian principle than any other opera-composer before 1893, save Wagner alone;* he has even gone to as great lengths as Wagner himself. Had he not done so, we

---

of Germany, till after the first and second Bayreuth years—1876 and 1882. *Tristan* in particular long hung fire with the public. It will be noticed that Roeder makes no mention of anything by Wagner later than *Lohengrin* being studied in Milan in the early 'seventies.

* Mere flashes in the pan, like Adalbert von Goldschmidt's *Helianthus* (Leipzig, 1884), do not count.

should hardly hear hard-and-fast Shaksperians (not even making allowance for the difference between Opera and spoken Drama) call Mr. Victor Maurel the greatest Iago and Falstaff they ever saw on any stage. Had Verdi's formula not been intrinsically Wagnerian, or his practice not true to his formula, no singing actor under the sun could have done in these parts what Maurel did.

For years Verdi's chief follower in Italy was Amilcare Ponchielli (born at Paderno Fasolaro, near Cremona, in 1834; died in Milan in 1886). Ponchielli died too early to follow Verdi in his latest direction, as he doubtless would have done; he reflected rather the influence of the works of the master's third period,—*La forza del destino, Don Carlos,*—which influence, in so far as it was specific, was mainly French. His creative power was considerable, he was decidedly a man of genius, if of the second rank; if he lacked Verdi's vigour of temperament,* he had a fine dramatic gift, and his technical musicianship was rather in advance of his day

---

* In this one respect, Ponchielli fell behind Errico Petrella (born in Palermo in 1813; died in Genoa in 1877), in all others, markedly his inferior. Petrella was Verdi's most noteworthy imitator in his earlier period; his *Ione, ossia l'ultimo giorno di Pompeji* (Milan, 1855) crossed the Italian frontier and even made its way to this country

in Italy. Of his ten completed operas, *La Gio-
conda* (the libretto by Arrigo Boïto; Milan,
1878) was best known outside of his native
country; it made the round of the musical
world—thanks partly to the music, partly to
Boïto's admirable text.

Next to Verdi's latest operas is to be mentioned the *Mefistofele* of Arrigo Boïto—the librettist of *Otello* and *Falstaff* (born in Padua in
1842). This work (first produced in Milan in
1868, then, largely rewritten, in Bologna in
1875) already shows a decided advance in the
modern direction over Verdi's *Aïda;* there are
scenes in it which anticipate a good deal in
Otello and *Falstaff* in the way of purely dramatic writing.*

Of the latest developments of Italian Opera
little that is definite can be said yet; Verdi's
last manner is recognizably the model, but this
whole neo-Italian movement is still too young,
too contemporary, to be summed up with any
approach to finality. Probably the man whom
the Italians themselves look upon as their
strongest to-day is Giacomo Puccini (born at

---

* It is, upon the whole, not easy to determine Boïto's place as
an Italian Wagnerian; since *Mefistofele*, he has produced nothing,
and *Mefistofele* reflects the Wagner influence only up to *Lohengrin*. One anxiously awaits the production of his long-promised
Nero to show where he really stands to-day.

Lucca in 1858). After producing several operas with varying success, he became known outside of Italy by his *La Bohème* (the text after Henri Murger's play ; Turin, 1896); how well the success of this work has been followed up by his *La Tosca* (after Sardou ; Rome, 1900) it is now too early to judge. Indisputably a man of no ordinary talent, Puccini can certainly rank with the best in Italy as a musician.*

Worthy of mention also, as among the newest of the new whose works have crossed both Alps and ocean, are Nicola Spinelli (born in Turin in 1865) † and Umberto Giordano (born

---

* Up to 1896, Puccini's career was unduly overshadowed by the flaming European success of Mascagni and Leoncavallo ; a circumstance at which Italian musicians of the better class were considerably scandalized. Not many years ago, the author heard one of them say : "It is a disgrace to our reputation abroad that immature and absolutely second-rate talents, like Mascagni and Leoncavallo, should be taken all over Europe as the foremost representatives of Italian Music to-day, while solid musicians, like Puccini and one or two others, are utterly unknown outside of their native country.

† *Labilia* (second Sonzogno prize in Milan, 1890, Mascagni's *Cavalleria* taking the first); *A basso porto* (first brought out in German at Cologne in 1894 ; then in the original Italian in several Italian cities ; then in German in Leipzig, 1899; in English, New York, 1900—judging from accounts, the most blood-thirsty piece on record !). *Vide* Mr. W. J. HENDERSON, in *The Musical Record* for March, 1900, page 107.

in Naples in 1869?); * but these are too young for their talent and standing to be estimated at all.

In Germany no such prominent instance of surrender to the Wagner influence as Verdi is yet to be noted. Some few of the younger men—Engelbert Humperdinck (born in 1854), Eugen d'Albert (1864), Richard Strauss (1864), etc.—have gone rather tentatively to considerable lengths in the Wagnerian direction; but none of them can fairly be said to have fully made his mark yet in Opera. On the other hand, a certain pseudo-Wagnerian influence—really nothing more than a *Nibelungen* influence—has made itself felt at times, in the way of inciting composers to write series of connected operas; August Bungert (born at Mühlheim-on-the-Ruhr in 1846), for instance, has laid out and partly written a hexalogy, *Homerische Welt*, several of the separate "evenings" of which have already been given.† But, judging from what accounts have come to this

---

* *Mala vita* (Rome, 1892; reproduced with great success, as *Il voto*, Milan, 1897); *Andrea Chenier* (Milan, 1896; New York, 1897); *Fedora* (after Sardou; Milan, 1898).

† This work consists of two main parts, *Die Ilias* and *Die Odyssee*. The former comprises the operas *Achilles* and *Klytemnestra*; the latter, the operas *Kirke*, *Nausikaa*, *Odysseus Heimkehr*, and *Odysseus Tod*. *Die Odyssee* was finished in 1896; *Die Ilias* is still unfinished.

country, the serial idea is all that is in any way Wagnerian in the work.*

The most successful men in Germany have gone over from Weber to Meyerbeer, rather than to Wagner; in Grand Opera of a rather modernized Meyerbeer type some brilliant things have been done. In this vein at least two men have made their mark : Anton Rubinstein (1830–1894) and Karl Goldmark (1830– still living). To be sure, Rubinstein's reputation as an opera-writer has never been more than *d'estime ;* but his *Der Thurm zu Babel* (Königsberg, 1870), *Nero* (Hamburg, 1879), and one or two others have made the round of Germany, or even crossed the frontier. Goldmark's success has been decidedly more ge-

---

* The serial opera mania broke out with some virulence in Germany shortly after the first Bayreuth year, 1876, but never came to much in the way of practical results. Mr. Arthur Nikisch used to tell hair-raising stories of MS. scores of tetralogies, pentalogies, and even a heptalogy, that were sent in for his approval when he was conductor at the Leipzig Stadt-Theater (before coming to America in 1889), "with interlude-music on *Leitmotiven* all written out for brass instruments, *à la* Bayreuth." He said, too, that he was by no means the only conductor in Germany who had been subjected to this infliction. None of those wonderful scores seems, however, to have seen the light of the lamps.

After all, the serial idea is not distinctively Wagnerian; Berlioz wrote his *Les Troyens*—a serial work, consisting of two connected operas, *La prise de Troie* and *Les Troyens à Carthage*—as early as 1856–63.

nuine; his *Die Königin von Saba* (Vienna, 1875) still outranks all but Wagner's operas in point of popularity and general esteem. His *Merlin* (1888) was not quite so well received. Still, Goldmark is unquestionably the most notable opera-composer in Germany to-day. It would, however, be a bold man who should predict that either *Nero* or *Die Königin von Saba* would ever work itself into so warm a place in the hearts of the German people, or have as long a life on the stage, as Marschner's *Templer und Jüdin* or *Hans Heiling*— both of which are pretty nearly dead by this time.

If Verdi came to Wagner through Meyerbeer, this is doubly true of the present French composers. The progress of Opera in France, since Gounod, has been marked by a gradual stretching of the Meyerbeer formula in the Wagnerian direction. Until very recently it had not reached the snapping-point; but it had, for years, been stretched and stretched until little of its original semblance was left. Exactly how far this or that French composer may have carried the process is hard to tell. No adequate idea of a modern opera can be formed from a pianoforte-score; one must either hear the work itself, or study the full score. Exceedingly few modern French operas have been given in this country ; and full scores are all but impossible to procure.* Even contemporary French accounts are confusing; the term " Wagnerian " is used very loosely; it may mean this or that, according to the writer. Moreover, the French operatic movement of the last two decades has led to such very new developments that its true value, even its true character, can hardly be justly estimated to-day, even in France.

This much may, however, be plausibly evolved: that the French have, as usual, been considerably theory-bound in their operatic do-ings for the last quarter of a century ; far more so than the Germans or Italians. Their racial infatuation for Logic, their profound respect for a scheme, or plan, have stood much in the way of their going to work naïvely and in-stinctively in their recent musical production.

---

* Few persons, outside the musical profession, have any idea of the difficulty of procuring modern opera-scores, especially French and Italian ones. Publishers hang on to them like grim Death. Some notion of this difficulty may be formed from the fact that the full score of Bizet's *L'Arlésienne* (the first orchestral suite) is not to be bought to-day for love or money, but only hired. A few years ago, a French publisher offered a collector — note, a collector; not a conductor or manager—twenty-five full scores of modern French operas for 12,500 francs ($2,500), and would not hear of letting anything less than the whole collection of twenty-five go! Even opportunities like this are rare.

Nearly everything they have done has been done with a fixed intent, and, especially of late years, have the Opera and Music in general been to them problems—to be solved intellectually. One is almost forced to the conclusion that no man of really commanding musical genius has appeared in French Music since Berlioz; * no man who, by simply following his star, could find himself in a new path, without preconceived plan. No doubt the same may be said of Germany and Italy; but neither of these countries has been so fruitful in brand-new developments in Opera as France has of late. Ever since the Wagner influence began to tell, France has evinced a burning thirst for progress in Music; but it has tried to slake this thirst with pure inventiveness, by seeking to discover new paths with malice prepense, and, as it were, by precalculating originality.

Since Gounod, French opera-composers may roughly be divided into two classes: those who try to be as Wagnerian as they can, and still remain French; those who try to be as progressive as they can, without being Wagnerian.

* César Franck alone is probably to be excepted here; but he does not come within the pale of a history of Opera. Furthermore, Franck was a Belgian; having, to be sure, many affiliations with the French school, but of un-Gallic, Flemish blood.

One might think these two aims very like two stools, between which a national Art was in some danger of coming to the ground. Wagner is, after all, at the heart of the matter; to get at the Future by steering round him, or by working a passage through him and out on the other side—these are the problems that have occupied musical France for the last two decades, and longer.

Since Gounod died, in 1893, the potentate of French Grand Opera, the "King of the Académie de Musique," has been Jules Massenet (born at Montaud, Loire, in 1842).* Camille Saint-Saëns (born in Paris in 1835) may be said to run him hard, but has never quite won his popularity and influence.† Among the more determined Wagnerians at the Académie de Musique may be mentioned Ernest Reyer (born in Marseilles in 1823), Gervais-Bernard Salvayre (born at Toulouse in 1847) and Emmanuel Chabrier (born at Ambert, Puy-de-Dôme, in 1841; died in Paris in 1894).‡

---

* Massenet's grand operas have been: *Le Roi de Lahore* (Paris, 1877), *Hérodiade* (Brussels, 1881), *Le Cid* (Paris, 1885), *Le Mage* (ibid., 1891), and *Thaïs* (ibid., 189⬛).

† Saint-Saëns has produced in Grand Opera *Samson et Dalila* (Weimar, 1877), *Étienne Marcel* (Lyons, 1879), *Henry VIII* (Paris, 1883), and *Ascanio* (ibid., 1890).

‡ Reyer's *Sigurd* was brought out at the Académie de Musique

But more interesting than any recent developments in Grand Opera is the course pursued
by French *opéra-comique* since this eminently
" national" form received its first hard blow
from Offenbach *opéra-bouffe* in the 'fifties.* The
first effect was to throw *opéra-comique* into a
more serious path, thus veiling all semblance
of competition between it and its jaunty young
rival. With Meyerbeer's *Étoile du Nord* (1854)
and *Le Pardon de Ploërmel* (1859), it had already
begun to approach the form of Grand Opera—
in extensive musical developments, in reducing
the spoken dialogue to the smallest practicable proportions. This tendency was equally
marked in Gounod's *Mireille* (1864), Ambroise
Thomas's *Mignon* (1866), and Georges Bizet's
matchless *Carmen* (1875).† Indeed, Meyerbeer,
Gounod, Thomas, and Bizet brought French
opéra-comique—as far as regards scheme, or plan

---

in 1885 ; Salvayre's *La Dame de Monsoreau*, in 1888 ; Chabrier's
Gwendoline, in 1893. The latter work was first given in Brussels
in 1886, and has since been given in Carlsruhe (1889), Munich
(1890), and Leipzig (1893, under Emil Paur).

* Offenbach, his works, and imitators form no part of our present subject ; suffice it that *opéra-bouffe* did deal *opéra-comique* a
severe blow, distracting public attention from the more " legiti-
mate" form for a time, not only in Paris, but all over France.

† Thomas was born at Metz in 1811, and died in Paris in
1896 ; Alexandre-César-Léopold (*dit* Georges) Bizet was born in
Paris in 1838, and died at Bougival in 1875.

—up to the level of the larger forms of the German *Spieloper*, as treated by Beethoven, Spohr, and Weber. The spoken dialogue is the merest indispensable connecting thread between the musical numbers, which latter occupy the first place, and are often developed in a way, and to an extent, that would do no shame to Grand Opera.

This direction has been pursued still farther by Léo Delibes, in his *Jean de Nivelle* (1880) and *Lakmé* (1883); Victor Massé, in *Une nuit de Cléopâtre* (1885); Victorin de Joncières, in *Le Chevalier Jean* (1885); Massenet, in *Manon* (1884), *Esclarmonde* (1889), *Werther* (1893), and *Sapho* (1897); Benjamin Godard, in *Dante* (1890); Saint-Saëns, in *Proserpine* (1887) and *Phryné* (1893); and, above all, by Édouard Lalo, in his *Le Roi d' Ys* (1888), which last work probably reaches the highest level of modern *opéra-comique*.* In some of these operas the spoken dialogue disappears entirely; when we come to

---

* Léo Delibes was born at Saint-Germain-du-Val, Sarthe, in 1836, and died in Paris in 1891.

Victor Massé was born at Lorient, Morbihan, in 1822, and died in Paris in 1884.

Victorin de Joncières was born in Paris in 1839.

Benjamin Godard was born in Paris in 1849, and died at Cannes in 1895.

Édouard Lalo was born at Lille in 1823, and died in Paris in 1892.

the extreme modern men (of whom more later), we find that this is the rule. The distinction between Grand Opera and *opéra-comique* is no longer one of plan.*

If the Wagner influence has been more or less fruitfully felt everywhere, one reaction against it—or rather against one phase of Wagner's example—is noteworthy. This is the reaction against what might be called "sea-serpent" operas.† The writing of exceedingly long operas was not begun by Wagner; he only outdid most of his predecessors in that line. The original sinners were the composers for the Académie de Musique in Paris, Meyerbeer being, if not the first, certainly the chief of them. Opera-goers in this country can hardly have a notion of the length of such works as *Les Huguenots* or *L'Africaine*, when given without cuts; even when given as they are in Paris, with far fewer cuts than here. Wagner excused the in-

---

* It should be said that the term *opéra-comique* is not used on the title-pages of many of the more modern works; the designations *drame-lyrique*, or *comédie-lyrique*, are quite as common. But it has been thought best, for the sake of simplicity, to retain the older term here, as indicating an opera written for, and brought out at the Théâtre de l'Opéra-Comique in Paris. It will be remembered that, for many years, this term has not necessarily implied anything of a comic character.

† "Composers nowadays write veritable sea-serpent concertos, of enormous length!"—HANS VON BÜLOW.

ordinate length of his *Rienzi* on the ground of its having been originally written for Paris, " for a public that did not take supper." * But the *Meistersinger* is fully as long as *Les Huguenots* (if not still longer), and has no Parisian excuse to show for it! And, when we come to the four days of the *Nibelungen*, or Bungert's *Odysseus*, we have the " sea-serpent Opera " in its fullest bloom.

The first reaction, or protest, came from Italy —where Wagner's *Ring* had become sufficiently known by that time—in 1890, in the shape of Mascagni's *Cavalleria rusticana*. This short two-act opera, with an orchestral *intermezzo* that makes the two acts go at a single sitting, had what managers call a phenomenal success; it flew all over Italy and Germany in a jiffy, and the thitherto unknown Mascagni became suddenly a seven-days' wonder, the hero of the hour. The *Cavalleria* was followed, and its success capped, in 1892, by Leoncavallo's

---

* When Wagner used to conduct this opera, as court Kapellmeister, in Dresden in the 'forties, the first two acts were given on one evening, and the third, fourth, and fifth on the next.

The French mania for very long theatrical and musical entertainments is verily fit to make one stare! What think you of this program of a Conservatoire concert? Mozart's G minor symphony, the whole of Saint-Saëns's *Déluge* (an oratorio in three parts), and Beethoven's C minor symphony. The author sat through this, one Sunday afternoon in 1891.

Pagliacci, another work of the same dimensions.*

Cavalleria rusticana and *Pagliacci* soon made the round of the musical world. Of course the composers were hailed at first as epoch-making geniuses ; then (though not necessarily of course) they turned out to be mere flashes in the pan. Both men seem to have written themselves out at the first dash ; for neither has been able to renew his maiden success.† What at first seemed genius was afterward found to be little, or nothing, more than that hap-hazard inspiration under which very third-rate men have at times produced one supremely good thing of its kind, and then flickered out in their sockets.‡ There can be no doubt that the music of *Cavalleria rusticana* and *Pagliacci* is thoroughly genuine, if not particularly well-written, stuff ; then, both libretti are admirable in their straightforward naturalism, though dripping with the ruddiest of gore.

The success of these two works was so over-

---

* Pietro Mascagni was born in Leghorn in 1863 ; Ruggiero Leoncavallo, in Naples in 1858.

† The report that Mascagni wrote the *Cavalleria* hurriedly, on the spur of the Sonzogno prize, turned out to be a canard ; the opera may have been quickly put together, but was largely a *pasticcio* of music which Mascagni had been years in writing.

‡ Rouget de Lisle's *La Marseillaise* and, in a less degree, Karl Wilhelm's *Die Wacht am Rhein* are instances of this.

whelming, moreover, their shortness was so clearly an element of it, that Germany could not be long in following the Italian lead—Germany, a supper-eating country that could tell Italy the most pitiful tales of "sea-serpent operas" interfering with its favourite indulgence! But the blood-curdling atrocities of *Cavalleria* and *Pagliacci* were not to be repeated by a nation possessed of a sense of humour ; if Germany was to chime in with Italy's reactionary protest against four- and five-hour operas, she must at least show the originality of herself reacting against the sensational blood-thirstiness of the Italian example. So, for carnal exuberance and murder, Germany would substitute the charm of her own *Mährchen* folk-lore ; a fertile field which Opera had, somehow, long forgotten to exploit. In December, 1893,—not quite two years after *Pagliacci*,— Engelbert Humperdinck (born at Siegburg-on-the-Rhine, near Bonn, in 1858) came out triumphantly with his *Hänsel und Gretel;* which lead was followed two years later, in 1896, by Goldmark in Vienna with his *Das Heimchen am Herd* (the libretto adapted from Dickens's *Cricket on the Hearth*). These two little operas also made the rounds of musical Europe ; the opera-going world is awaiting more of the same sort.

Two still newer departures in Opera, and of

quite another character, are to be noted in France. The first of these was made almost simultaneously by Alfred Bruneau (born in Paris in 1857) and Vincent d'Indy (born ibid. in 1851); it was nothing more nor less than writing an opera to a prose libretto.* In 1897 Bruneau's *Messidor*, the prose text by Émile Zola, was brought out at the Académie de Musique; it was followed in 1898, at the Opéra-Comique, by d'Indy's *Fervaal*, the last word, so far, of French Wagnerianism, the text in "rhythmic prose." † In how far this example, which has certainly something to be said for it,

---

*Native French composers had long felt the difficulty of fitting music, with its infinite variety of rhythms, to the regular iambic or trochaic metre of French verse—a matter which gave that Gallicized German, Offenbach, no qualms of conscience whatever. As far back as 1820, Castil-Blaze came out with a pamphlet arraigning composers for the liberties they took with French verse in their vocal writing; Berlioz, on the other hand, sharply called the poets to account for writing verse that was unfit for good musical setting; no French poet, not even the finical Racine, making any bones of an ear-scorching *hiatus* between the last syllable of a line and the first of the next, which *hiatus* would become perfectly apparent in the midst of musical phrase.

† This "rhythmic prose" is something like what Jean Paul calls the *Streckvers*, or blank verse of indefinite length. John Bunyan falls into much the same vein in parts of his *Pilgrim's Progress*, as does also Dante in the *Vita nuova*. Probably the finest modern examples of this sort of thing are to be found in Gustave Flaubert's *Salammbô* and *La Tentation de Saint-Antoine*.

will be followed in future, remains to be seen. Bruneau has shown himself a come-outer in other ways, too; it is to him that the world owes the conception of the *opéra naturaliste*, as exemplified in his *L'Attaque du Moulin* (Opéra-Comique, 1893); a work in which the naturalistic idea does not, however, seem to be pushed essentially farther than in Mascagni's *Cavalleria* or Leoncavallo's *Pagliacci*.

The other, and newest, departure has just been made by Gustave Charpentier (born at Dieuze, Lorraine, in 1860) in his *Louise* (Opéra-Comique, 1900); here the composer turns over an entirely original leaf. Unlike Wagner, who avowedly made his orchestra give a sort of running emotional commentary on the action and incidents of the drama (like the ancient Greek chorus), Charpentier confines his orchestra to a suggestive painting of the *milieu*, or surroundings, in which the action takes place. As the action of *Louise* passes in the Montmartre district of Paris, Bruneau has "put all Montmartre, all Paris into his orchestra"— hawkers' cries, the tunes played by itinerant venders on shrill-piping instruments, familiar street-noises, and what not else. Of what the *dramatis personæ* themselves are doing, the orchestra takes comparatively little heed. This may be regarded as the last-spoken word in modern Opera; what weight it may have, what echoes it may evoke in the future, heaven only knows.*

---

* Concerning this *Louise* of Charpentier's, *vide* Miss IRENE DAVIS, in *The Musical Record* for March, 1900, page 110.

FINIS.

APPENDIX

PERI'S PREFACE TO *EURIDICE*

To my Readers :—

Before offering you (kind Readers) this music of mine, I think proper to make known to you what led me to invent this new kind of vocal writing ; since reason must be the beginning and source of all human doings, and he who can not give his reason at once lays himself open to the suspicion of having worked at hap-hazard. Although our music was brought upon the stage by Sig. Emilio del Cavaliere, with marvellous originality, before anyone else I know of, it nevertheless pleased Signori Iacopo Corsi and Ottavio Rinuccini (in the year 1594) to have me set to music the play of *Dafne*, written by Sig. Ottavio Rinuccini, treating it in another manner, to show by a simple experiment of what the song of our age is capable. Wherefore, seeing that I had to do with Dramatic Poetry, and must accordingly seek, in my music, to imitate one who speaks (and doubtless no one ever yet spoke in singing), it seemed to me that the ancient Greeks and Romans (who, in the opinion of many, sang the whole of their tragedies on the stage) must have made use of a sort of music which, while surpassing the sounds of ordinary speech, fell so far short of the melody of singing as to assume the shape of something intermediate between the two. And this is why we find in their poems so large an use made of the Iambic Metre, which does not rise to the sublimity of the Hexameter, albeit it is said to overstep the bounds of ordinary speech. Therefore, abandoning every style of vocal writing known hitherto, I gave myself up wholly to contriving the sort of imitation [of speech] demanded by this poem. And, considering that the sort of vocal delivery applied by the ancients to singing, and called by them *vox diastematica* (as if held in check and kept in suspense), could be somewhat accelerated, so as to hold a mean course between the slow and deliberate pace of singing and the nimble, rapid pace of speaking, and thus be made to serve my purpose (as they, too, adapted it to the reading of poems and heroic verse) by approaching the speaking voice, called by them *vox continuata*, as has also been done by our modern composers (if perhaps for another purpose) ; considering this, I also recognized that, in our speech, some sounds are intoned in such a way that harmony can be based upon them,* and that, in the course of conversation, we pass through many others which are not so intoned, until we return to one which is capable of forming a new consonance. And, having regard for the accents and modes of expression we use—in grief, rejoicing, etc.—I have made the bass move at

---

* It will be seen that Peri here has in mind that sort of sing-song which is a prominent characteristic of ordinary Italian speech.

a rate appropriate to them, now faster, now slower, according to the emotions to be expressed, and have sustained it through both dissonances and consonances (*tra le false, e tra le buone proporzioni*), until the speaker's voice, after passing through various degrees of pitch, comes to those sounds which, being intoned in ordinary speech, facilitate the formation of a new consonance. And I have done this not only to the end that the vocal delivery shall neither wound the ear (as if stumbling in meeting with repeated chords or too frequent consonances) nor seem, as it were, to dance to the movement of the bass, especially in sad or grave passages which naturally call for others in a more lively and rapid movement, but also to the end that the employment of dissonances shall diminish, or conceal that advantage * which is increased by having to intone every note—an advantage of which ancient music may perhaps have had less need. And finally (though I dare not assert that this was the sort of singing done in the Greek and Roman plays), I have deemed it the only sort that can be admissible in our music, by adapting itself to our speech.

For this reason I communicated my opinion to those Gentlemen ; I showed them this new manner of singing, and it pleased them most highly—not only Sig. Iacopo, who had already composed very beautiful airs for the same play, but Sig. Pietro Strozzi, Sig. Francesco Cini, and other gentlemen

---

* *I.e.*, the advantage of having a bass to sing to.

well up in the subject (for music flourishes amongst
the nobility to-day), as well as that famous artist
who may be called the Euterpe of our age, Signora
Vettoria (*sic*) Archilei, one who has always made my
music worthy of her singing by adorning it, not only
with those turns and long vocal flourishes (*di quei
gruppi, e di quei lunghi giri di voce*), both simple and
double, which are at all times devised by the activity
of her genius,—more in obedience to the fashion of
our time than because she thinks they constitute
the beauty and strength of our singing,—but also
with those charms and graces which can not be
written down, and, when written, are not to be
learnt from the writing. It was heard and com-
mended by Messer. Giovanbattista Jacomelli, who
excels in every department of music, and has
almost exchanged surnames with the Violin,* on
which instrument he is admirable. And, for the
three successive years that it was given in Carnival-
time, it was heard with the greatest delight and
received with universal applause by everyone present. But the present *Euridice* had even better fortune ; not because it was heard by the Gentlemen,
and other men of worth, whom I have named, and
also by Sig. Conte Alfonso Fontanella and Sig.
Orazio Vecchi, most noble witnesses to my idea, but
because it was performed before so great a Queen
and so many famous Princes of Italy and France,
and was sung by the most excellent musicians of

---

* He was known as Giovanbattista dal Violino.

our time; of whom Sig. Francesco Rosi (*sic*), a
nobleman of Arezzo, took the part of Aminta*; Sig.
Antonio Brandi, that of Arcetro; and Sig. Melchior
Palantrotti, that of Plutone; and, behind the scenes,
the music was played by gentlemen illustrious for
nobility of blood or excellence in music: Sig. Iacopo
Corsi, whom I have so often mentioned, played a
gravicembalo; Sig. Don Grazia Montalvo, a chitar-
rone; Messer. Gio. Battista dal Violino, a lira
grande; Messer. Giov. Lupi, a liuto grosso. And,
although I had then written it exactly in the shape
in which it is now published, nevertheless Giulio
Caccini (called Romano), whose supreme worth is
known to the World, wrote the air of Euridice and
some of those of the Pastore and the Ninfa del Coro,
beside the choruses " *Al canto, al ballo*," " *Sospirate*,"
and "*Poichè gli eterni imperi*"; and this because
they were to be sung by persons dependent upon
him. Which airs may be read in his score, composed, however, and printed after this of mine had
been performed before Her Most Christian Majesty.

Receive it, therefore, kindly, courteous readers,
and, though I may not, this time, have reached the
point I thought myself able to reach (regard for
novelty having been a curb on my course), accept it
graciously in every way. And perhaps it will come to

---

* Francesco Rasi was a singer attached to Vincenzo Gonzaga
in Mantua; this, and his taking part in the performance of *Euridice*, may account for the Florentine operatic lead being first
followed at the Mantuan court.

pass on another occasion that I shall show you something more perfect than this. Meanwhile, I shall think to have done enough if I have opened the path for the talent of others, for them to walk in my foot-steps to that glory to which it has not been given to me to attain. And I hope that my use of dissonances, played and sung discreetly, yet without timidity (having pleased so many and worthy men), will not trouble you ; especially in the sad and grave airs of Orfeo, Arcetro, and Dafne—which part was taken with much grace by Iacopo Giusti, a young boy from Lucca. And may you live happy.

FLORENCE, February 6, 1600.

GLUCK'S PREFACE TO *ALCESTE*

Your Royal Highness :—

When I undertook to compose the music to *Alceste*, my intention was to rid it of all those abuses which, introduced either through the mistaken vanity of singers or the over-indulgence of composers, have so long disfigured Italian Opera, and turned the finest and most pompous spectacle into the most ridiculous and tedious. I wished to reduce music to its true function, which is to second poetry in expressing the emotions and situations of the play, without interrupting the action nor chilling it with useless and superfluous ornaments, and I believed that music ought to be to poetry what vividness of colouring and well-managed contrasts of light and shade are to a correct and well-composed drawing, serving to animate the figures without marring the outline. I accordingly have wished neither to stop an actor where the dialogue is at its warmest, in order to let the orchestra play a tedious *ritornello*, nor to hold him back on a favourable vowel in the middle of a word, that he may either show off the agility of his fine voice in a long roulade or wait for the orchestra to give him time to take breath for a cadenza. I have not thought proper to pass rapidly over the second part of an air, even when it is the more important and passionate, so as to repeat the words of the first part the regulation four times, and end the air where the sense perhaps does not end, to give the singer an easy opportunity to show that he can capriciously vary a passage in as many different ways; in fine, I have sought to banish all those abuses against which common sense and reason have so long protested in vain.

I have deemed that the overture ought to apprize the spectator of the action to be represented, and, so to speak, constitute itself the argument; that the coöperation of the instruments should be determined proportionately to the interest and passion [of a scene], and that no sharp contrasts between air and recitative should be left in the dialogue, so as not to stunt the period out of all reason, nor inappropriately interrupt the vigour and warmth of the action.

I have believed, furthermore, that my greatest efforts should be reduced to seeking for a beautiful simplicity, and have avoided making a display of difficulties, to the prejudice of clearness; the discovery of a novelty has not seemed admirable in my eyes, except in so far as it was naturally suggested by the situation, or helpful to the expression; and there is no rule of form which I have not thought best willingly to sacrifice to the effect.

Such are my principles. Fortunately the libretto lent itself marvellously well to my purpose; the

celebrated author, having imagined a new scheme
for the drama, had substituted the language of the
heart, strong passions, interesting situations, and an
ever-varied spectacle for flowery descriptions, superfluous metaphors, and cold and sententious moral-
izing.* Success has already vindicated my maxims,
and the universal approbation of so enlightened a
city has shown clearly that simplicity, truth, and
naturalness are the prime principles of beauty in all
productions of art. Still, notwithstanding repeated
urging from most respectable persons, seeking to
induce me to publish my work in print, I have felt
all the risk one runs in combating such general and
deeply - rooted prejudices, and have found myself
under the necessity of being assured of Your Royal
Highness's most powerful patronage, imploring the
favour of engraving, at the head of my work, your
August Name, which unites the suffrages of enlightened Europe with so much reason. The great Pro-
tector of the fine-arts, reigning over a nation which
has had the glory of raising them up from under
universal oppression, and of producing in each of
them the greatest models, in a city which has always
been the first to cast off the yoke of vulgar prejudice, to open for itself a way leading to perfection,
He alone can undertake the reformation of that
noble spectacle in which all the arts have so large a

---

* Shades of the *Camerata!* and this is how Gluck treats your
sacrosanct Euripides !—W. F. A.

share. If You succeed in this, the glory of having laid the first stone will remain to me, and also this public testimony to Your high Protection ; for which favour I have the honour to declare myself with the most humble respect,

Y. R. H.'s

Most humble, Most devoted, Most obliged Servant,

CHRISTOPHE GLUCK.*

* This preface is addressed to Leopold II., Grand-Duke of Tuscany.

INDEX

231

Index

232

Index

Index

Index

Index

THE MUSIC LOVER'S LIBRARY

THE MUSIC LOVER'S LIBRARY

JUST PUBLISHED

Choirs and Choral Music

By ARTHUR MEES

Conductor of the New York Mendelssohn Glee Club.

With 8 portraits and other illustrations.   12mo, $1.25 *net.*

CONTENTS

A concise account of the development of choirs and choral music from the earliest times to the present day, including brief popular expositions of the principal choral forms, interesting facts concerning notable performances of favorite oratorios, the history of celebrated choirs, and practical observations on the conduct of choral organizations.

Index

Index